EASY KANJI

A Basic Guide to Writing Japanese Characters

By Fujihiko Kaneda

Calligraphy by Masaya Katayama and Rika Sagano

Advised by Takuya Dan

PASSPORT BOOKS

NTC/Contemporary Publishing Company

Also available
Easy Hiragana
Easy Katakana

Cover design by Takashi Suzuki
Pen calligraphy by Masaya Katayama
Brush calligraphy by Rika Sagano

Originally published by Yohan Publications, Inc.

This edition first published in 1996 by Passport Books
A division of NTC/Contemporary Publishing Group, Inc.
4255 West Touhy Avenue, Lincolnwood (Chicago), Illinois 60712-1975 U.S.A.
Printed in the United States of America
International Standard Book Number: 0-8442-8374-6

  7 8 9 10 VRS/VRS 0 4 3 2 1

CONTENTS

Author's Preface ·   1

Introduction ·   3

Basic Strokes for Writing Kanji · · · · · · · · · · · · · · ·   7

Stroke Orders for Writing Kanji · · · · · · · · · · · · · · 19

Important Stroke Orders · 28

Chapter 1 · 32

Various Handwriting Styles of *Kanji* and *Kana* · · · · 32

How to Practice Writing *Kanji* · · · · · · · · · · · · · · · · 33

  1. "People" group characters · · · · · · · · · · · · · · · · · · 34

  2. "Tree" group characters · 35

  3. "Day" group characters · 36

  4. "Sweeping stroke" group characters · · · · · · · · · · · 37

  5. "Pot lid" group characters · · · · · · · · · · · · · · · · · · 38

  6. "Grass crown" group characters · · · · · · · · · · · · · · 39

      Exercise 1 · 40

  7. "Water" group characters · · · · · · · · · · · · · · · · · · · 42

  8. "Roof" group characters · · · · · · · · · · · · · · · · · · · 43

  9. "Tree with pent roof" group characters · · · · · · · · · · 44

 10. "Speak" group characters · · · · · · · · · · · · · · · · · · · 45

 11. "Ground" group characters · · · · · · · · · · · · · · · · · · 46

 12. "Frame" group characters · · · · · · · · · · · · · · · · · · · 47

      Exercise 2 · 48

13. "Wide house" group characters ················ 50

14. "Thread" group characters ····················· 51

15. "Advance" group characters ···················· 52

16. "Door" group characters ······················· 53

17. "Scarecrow" group characters ················· 54

18. "Heart" group characters ····················· 55

     Exercise 3 ································· 56

19. "Fire" group characters ······················· 58

20. "Flame" group characters ······················ 59

21. "God" group characters························ 60

22. "Bow" group characters························ 61

23. "Rain" group characters ······················· 62

24. "Bamboo" group characters ·················· 63

     Exercise 4 ································· 64

25. "Ax" group characters ························· 66

26. "*Wa* on the top" group characters ············· 67

27. "*Sun*" group characters ······················ 68

28. "Stand" group characters ····················· 69

29. "Town" group characters ····················· 70

30. "Sickness" group characters ··················· 71

     Exercise 5 ································· 72

31. "Sheep" group characters ····················· 74

32. "Bird" group characters························ 75

33. "Chicken" group characters ·················· 76

34. "Mouth" group characters····················· 77

35. "Walk" group characters ····················· 78

36. "Animal" group characters ··················· 79

     Exercise 6 ································· 80

37. "Mountain" group characters ·················· 82
38. "Vehicle" group characters ··················· 83
39. "Stone" group characters ···················· 84
40. "Gate" group characters ···················· 85
41. "*U* on the top" group characters ·············· 86
42. "Child" group characters ···················· 87
    Exercise 7 ······························· 88
43. "Moon" group characters ···················· 90
44. "King" group characters ···················· 91
45. "Hole" group characters ···················· 92
46. "Look" group characters ···················· 93
47. "Ear" group characters ····················· 94
48. "Two feet" group characters ················· 95
    Exercise 8 ······························· 96
49. "Gold (Metal)" group characters ·············· 98
50. "Woman" group characters ·················· 99
51. "Hand" group characters ··················· 100
52. "Roof and two crossed lines" group characters ···· 101
53. "Big shell" group characters ················· 102
54. "Feather" group characters ·················· 103
    Exercise 9 ······························· 104
55. "Clothing" group characters ················· 106
56. "Small village" group characters ·············· 107
57. "Food" group characters ···················· 108
58. "Robe" group characters ···················· 109
59. "Rice field" group characters ················· 110
60. "Rice" group characters····················· 111
    Exercise 10 ······························ 112

61. "Direction" group characters ················· 114

62. "Eye" group characters ························ 115

63. "And" group characters························ 116

64. "Ship" group characters ····················· 117

65. "Two swords" group characters ··············· 118

66. "Standing heart" group characters ············ 119

      Exercise 11 ······························ 120

67. "Roof and left wing" group characters ·········· 122

68. "Cow" group characters ····················· 123

69. "Shell" group characters ····················· 124

70. "Horse" group characters ···················· 125

71. "Enclosed by three fences" group characters ······ 126

72. "Large" group characters ···················· 127

      Exercise 12 ····························· 128

73. "Open box" group characters ················· 130

74. "Muscle power" group characters ············· 131

75. "Running" group characters····················· 132

76. "Eight" group characters ····················· 133

77. "Flag" group characters ····················· 134

78. "Death" group characters ····················· 135

      Exercise 13 ······························ 136

79. "Human" group characters ··················· 138

80. "Ice" group characters ························ 139

81. "Wide open mouth" group characters ············ 140

82. "Three diagonal strokes" group characters ········ 141

83. "Weapon" group characters ··················· 142

84. "Small shelf on the top" group characters ········ 143

85. "Day" (variation) group characters ············· 144

86. "Stop" group characters ····················· 145

87. "Pike" group characters························ 146

88. More complicated characters (1) ·············· 147

89. More complicated characters (2) ·············· 148

90. More complicated characters (3) ·············· 149

    Exercise Sheet ····························· 150

Chapter 2 ····································· 151

Basic Hiragana ································ 152

Basic Katakana ································ 154

Short Sentences with Kanji···················· 156

Japanese Proverbs····························· 168

Addressing a Letter in Japanese ················ 179

New Year's Greeting Cards···················· 184

Sample Letter (to a Friend) ·················· 192

On Radicals and Their Meanings ··············· 198

    Exercise Sheets ··························· 205

✢✢✢✢✢✢✢✢✢✢✢✢✢✢✢✢✢✢✢✢✢✢✢

About the Authors

Fujihiko Kaneda, a graduate of Osaka University of Foreign Studies, is extremely interested in studying new methods of teaching Japanese to both serious foreign students and people who are interested in the Japanese language.

    Other books: Yohan English-Japanese, Japanese-English
                        Dictionary
                        Easy Hiragana
                        Fuji-Tokaido

Takuya Dan, the headmaster of Japan Dynamic Calligraphy Society, created a new, original and highly stylized calligraphy in 1967 by revising the older Japanese forms.

He has designed logos for many leading companies in Japan. His works have been shown at exhibitions in the major cities of the world.

    Other books: Dōsho (Dynamic Calligraphy)
                        Basic Textbook for Dynamic Calligraphy

Rika Sagano, whose real name is Toshiko Mikuriya, was born in Saga Prefecture. In 1981, she moved to Tokyo, drawn by the Dynamic Calligraphy of Takuya Dan, and joined his society while teaching traditional calligraphy at a calligraphy school. She is now one of the top leaders of the society, but still continues to teach traditional and practical calligraphy. Her works have been shown at numerous calligraphy exhibits both within and without Japan.

She wrote the characters by brush for this book and they are useful for readers to see the differences between brush calligraphy and pen calligraphy.

Masaya Katayama, born in Osaka, has produced many books as an editor, proofreader and translator. In addition to those pursuits he is also a student of practical calligraphy. He wrote the characters by pen for this book, and with these characters, readers will be able to understand each character's small and complicated details.

Author's Preface

After 3 years research, the final volume in the Easy Japanese Writing Series has finally been compiled in what I hope is a compact and easy-to-follow format.

Written Japanese consists of a combination of *kanji* (Chinese characters), *hiragana* and *katakana*. As explained in the previous books "Easy Katakana" and "Easy Hiragana", *katakana* and *hiragana* are phonetic symbols and represent pronunciation. *Hiragana* is used solely for expressing Japanese words whereas *katakana* is used to express foreign words, foreign names and loanwords.

To most foreigners, I imagine the task of mastering *kanji* must seem a very daunting project, one that only a genius would undertake. However, if approached in a methodical way it becomes merely a question of patience more than anything else.

With this concept in mind I have taken the *kanji* and broken them down into simple basic strokes. The key to this being that even the most complicated *kanji* is constructed of a simple, set stroke order that never varies.

I have composed this book so that the reader can systematically practice writing and reading skills, eventually being able to master 500 characters, and by combination, read 1000 words. The latter half of this book is comprised of practical Japanese sentences containing useful vocabulary using all three writing systems.

I believe if this book is used as it has been designed to be used, and if daily study is maintained, the student will be rewarded with a good solid base for studying *kanji* and be well on their way to reaching that light at the end of the tunnel.

Finally, I wish to express my deep appreciation to calligraphers Mr. Masaya Katayama and Ms. Rika Sagano for their invaluable help. Also many thanks to English advisers Ms. Gerardine Enright and Ms. Helen Forrest, for their patience and effort.

Additionally, I would like to thank Mr. Takuya Dan, headmaster of The Dynamic Calligraphy Society, for his invaluable advice with this project.

Fujihiko Kaneda

Introduction

Chinese characters were invented about 3,000 years ago to record the Chinese language, and have been in use throughout China since that time. However, there was still no written language in Japan during the same period. Traditions and skills necessary for survival were transmitted by word of mouth from generation to generation.

At this point in time, the Japanese had established separate small clans and within these clans there were a select few people known as *Katari-be*, who were responsible for passing on the history of the clan orally. As these clans were small, the nature of transactions between clan members was not yet complex and the need for a written language had not yet arisen.

However, around 2,000 years ago, as the techniques for agriculture and hunting greatly improved, the amount of trade, exchange and transfer of property rights between the clans also increased. In the meantime, some small clans united and others merged with much larger clans. The larger clans became increasingly powerful and they formed a tribal society — this further increased the range of associations and social intercourse. In the course of time their purely oral negotiations led to misunderstandings and confrontations and these resulted in tribal wars.

As the inadequacy of these oral negotiations became apparent, it became obvious that for such important matters as expressing one's intentions to associates in far off places, recording agreements, or passing on family and tribal history, a system of writing was necessary. There may well have been a system of pictographs in use at this time in Japan, but no substantial evidence of these prior to the arrival of *kanji* (Chinese characters) has been discovered.

In these years there were numerous violent conflicts and wars between the large tribes as they battled for political supremacy. Eventually, however, the strongest tribe took control, and in the 4th or 5th century Japan was established as a unified nation upon this rather unstable and volatile tribal alliance. For the first time a system of government was organized. At this time information regarding production levies and relevant documents for each tribe would only have been recorded in primitive pictographs if at all (although some schools of thought have it that *kanji* were transmitted from Korea at around this time).

Kanji had already been in use in China from ancient times, and noting its practicality, the rulers of ancient Japan decided to adopt this highly sophisticated writing style, and, with some modifications, to utilize it to record spoken Japanese. In effect, at this period, only a few educated people could read and write and transmit such things as the law, new discoveries and crucial events to each other.

The first Japanese to record their language originally attempted to read and write the Chinese using the same pronunciation as the Chinese. However their pronunciation continued to be a Japanized one as it was considerably difficult for them, given the intrinsic differences in the languages, to pronounce the characters with the Chinese intonation. To solve this problem the Japanese applied Japanese pronunciation to each respective character which had the same conceptual meaning. This is known as the *kun* (native Japanese)-reading. In some cases there was no suitable reading for the character in the Japanese language so the original *on* (Chinese-derived)-reading was used.

For example, the word 山 (mountain) in its *on*-reading is *'san'*, but the Japanese also applied the native *kun*-reading of *'yama'*. 海 (sea) is pronounced *'kai'* in its *on*-reading, but the Japanese also applied the native *kun*-reading of *'umi'*.

		kun-reading	*on*-reading
火	(fire)	*hi*	*KA*
水	(water)	*mizu*	*SUI*
木	(tree)	*ki*	*MOKU*
土	(ground)	*tsuchi*	*DO*
日	(day)	*hi*	*NICHI*

In the 7th century many hitherto rebellious local tribes finally relinquished power to the government. The result of which was a strong centralized government which established the foundation of the nation as we know it today. Due to the establishment of a powerful administration governed by the noble classes in the capital, the need for these characters increased all the more. For setting down the law, arranging census registration, collecting levies, transportation of silk and iron from local production centers and holding national ceremonies and festivals, the characters became absolutely necessary in order for officers to record orders and instructions and perform operations smoothly.

The government also organized a local administrative system in each district and dispatched a governor from the capital. A national temple was also established in each district and a Buddhist priest, whose duty it was to spread Buddhist teachings throughout the country, was dispatched as the minister of each temple. Again, this increased the need for communication and documentation between the central government and the local governors and priests.

In the Tang dynasty (618–907), the Japanese government sent as many as nineteen diplomatic missions to China. Each delegation, numbering 250~500 members, consisted of an ambassador, officers, Buddhist priests, students, artists and craftsmen. In China they learned about the judicature, science, civil engineering techniques, architecture, the arts and Buddhism. These delegates, upon returning to Japan, brought with them the Chinese language and characters and taught this complex writing style all over Japan

In this book *on*-reading is shown in *CAPITALS* and *kun*-reading is shown in small italics. (Regarding the reading for each *kanji*; some of them can be read in both *on*-reading and *kun*-reading, some of them can only be read in one way and others can be read in two or three different ways, through *on*-reading or *kun*-reading.)

Basic Strokes for Writing Kanji

1 大   2 三   3 字   4 十千   5 中小

6 日国   7 山区   8 岡   9 即力   10 弓

11 和   12 者   13 今   14 子也   15 水

16 家   17 忌亡   18 巻光   19 心   20 成

7

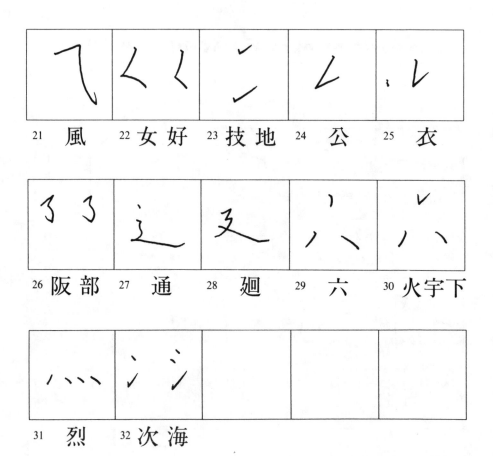

21　風　　22　女好　　23　技地　　24　公　　25　衣

26　阪部　　27　通　　28　廻　　29　六　　30　火字下

31　烈　　32　次海

Exercise: Practice writing the strokes. Join the dots to complete the strokes.

1. Long horizontal stroke

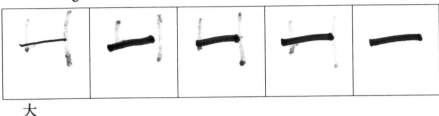

大

2. Short (above) and medium-length (below) horizontal strokes

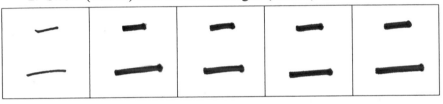

二 三

3. Horizontal stroke with downward flick at end

字 富

4. (a) Sword-like tapering vertical stroke with no pressure applied at the end (Pin point)
   (b) Medium-thickness vertical stroke with light pressure applied at the end (Dew drop)

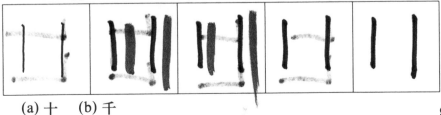

(a) 十   (b) 千

9

5. (a) Thick vertical stroke with pressure applied at the end
(Iron pole)

(b) Vertical stroke with upward flick at the end

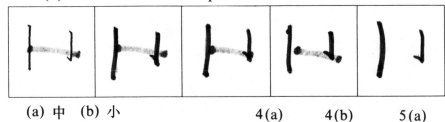

(a) 中 (b) 小   4(a)   4(b)   5(a)

The difference between these strokes (4(a), (b) and 5(a)) cannot be easily distinguished if written with a pen or pencil. To achieve the right effect a special writing brush must be used as shown on the right.

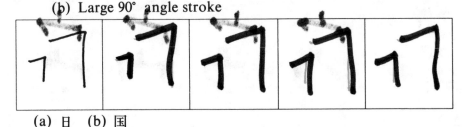

Kenshin   Suiro   Tetchu
(Pin point) (Dew drop) (Iron pole)

6. (a) Small 90° angle stroke

(b) Large 90° angle stroke

(a) 日 (b) 国

7. (a) Horizontal stroke joining a short vertical stroke at about a 90° angle

(b) Horizontal stroke joining a vertical stroke at a 90° angle

(a) 山 (b) 区

8. 90° angle stroke with flick at end

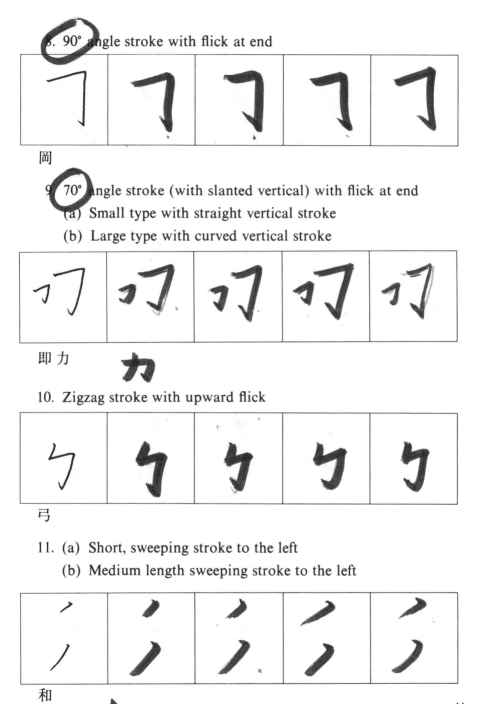

岡

9. 70° angle stroke (with slanted vertical) with flick at end

(a) Small type with straight vertical stroke

(b) Large type with curved vertical stroke

即 力

10. Zigzag stroke with upward flick

弓

11. (a) Short, sweeping stroke to the left

(b) Medium length sweeping stroke to the left

和

12. Long, sweeping stroke to the left

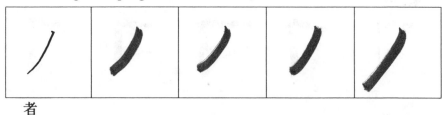

者

13. Sweeping stroke to the right

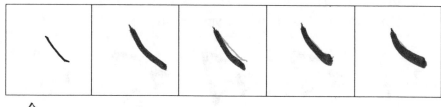

今

14. Short, acute-angled sweeping stroke (above)
   Long, acute-angled sweeping stroke (below)

子也

15. Short, slanted horizontal line with sweeping stroke

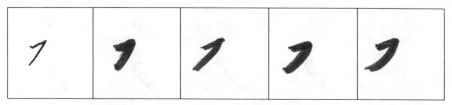

水

16. Curved vertical stroke with flick at the end

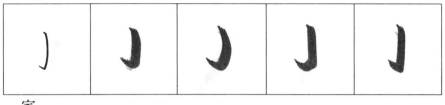

家

17. Short, curved 90° angle stroke without flick (above)
   Long, curved 90° angle stroke without flick (below)

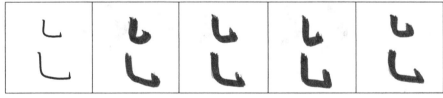

忌 亡

18. Short, curved 90° angle stroke with flick (above)
   Long, curved 90° angle stroke with flick (below)

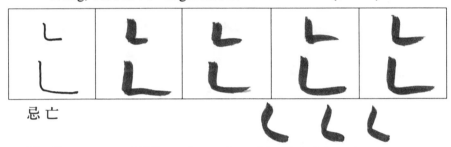

卷 光

19. Low-positioned fish hook stroke

心

20. Slightly-curved (slanted) vertical stroke with upward flick at the end

成

21. Slanted horizontal stroke joining curved vertical stroke with upward flick at the end

風

22. 90° left angle stroke (left)
    110° left angle stroke (right)

女 好

23. Small tick stroke (above) and medium length tick stroke (below)

技 地

24. Downward slanting stroke with a slightly rising
    horizontal stroke

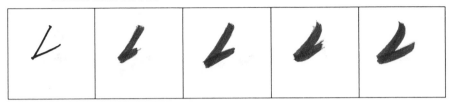

公

25. Vertical stroke with a tick at 50° degrees

衣

26. Ear-shaped stroke (left)   Ear-shaped stroke (right)

阪 部

(Note the differences in the above examples.)

27. Sweeping L-shaped stroke with the shortest stroke on the top

道

28. Right-sweeping, curved brush stroke, crossing elongated (3-shaped) stroke

延

The position of the stroke(s) of *Nyo*-group (See p. 30) occupies the left side and base of each *kanji* character.

29. *Ten* (1)

'*Ten*' means literally in Japanese 'a dot'. However, it should be considered as a kind of very short stroke or a variation thereof. There are strokes both long and short, pointing left and right, slanting, upwards and downwards in *kanji*.

(a) Short vertical stroke (above)

(b) Sweeping short stroke, slanting downwards to the left (below left)

(c) Short stroke slanting downwards to the right, stopping with pressure at the end (below right)

六

30. *Ten* (2)

    (a) Tick stroke (above)

    (b) Short stroke slanting downwards to left, stopping with pressure at the end (below left)

    (c) Short stroke slanting downwards to right, stopping with pressure at end (below right)

(a) 火 (b) 宇 (c) 下

The difference between the short strokes #29-c and #30-c can not be easily distinguished if written with a pen or pencil.

To achieve the right effect a special writing brush must be used as shown below.

For your reference the main short strokes are shown below as written with a brush.

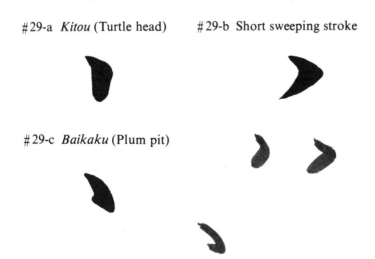

#29-a *Kitou* (Turtle head)   #29-b Short sweeping stroke

#29-c *Baikaku* (Plum pit)

17

#30-a Tick stroke

#30-b *Kyojin* (Apricot stone)

#30-c *Kaiseki* (Strange stone)

Choten (Long dot) a variation of
Kaiseki (#30-c)

#31 *Rekka* (Flame)

31. Four short strokes at the foot of a character

烈

32. One short stroke with small tick stroke (left)
Two short strokes with tick stroke (right)

次海

18

Stroke Orders for Writing Kanji

General guidelines for the correct way to write *kanji* are as follows:

The First Major Principle:

Draw from top to bottom.

Draw from the upper part to the lower part.

a) The stroke is drawn from the top point to the bottom point of the character.

b) Begin drawing the upper part of the character before drawing the lower part.

The Second Major Principle:

Draw from the left-hand side to the right-hand side.

Draw the left-hand section before drawing the right-hand section.

a) Begin drawing the character from the left-hand stroke.

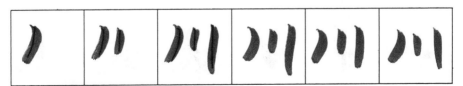

b) Draw the left-hand section of the character before the right-hand section.

Note: The left-hand radical is drawn before the body of the *kanji*. (This is the largest category of *kanji*.) Any *kanji* that can be divided into three sections is drawn from the left-hand side.

Minor Principles:

The first minor principle:

In the majority of cases, when the lines cross one another the horizontal line is drawn before the vertical line. (Refer to *the second minor principle* for exceptions to this rule.)

a) The stroke order of horizontal and vertical lines is as follows:

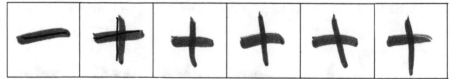

Even if the vertical line is curved after the crossing, draw the horizontal line first.

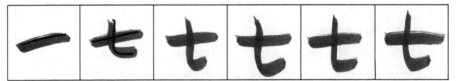

Even if other strokes are added to the main body of the *kanji*, the horizontal line is drawn first.

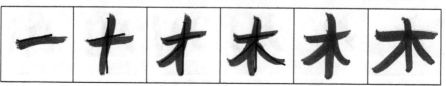

b) The stroke order in the case of one horizontal line and two vertical lines is as follows:

The top horizontal line is drawn first, followed by the two vertical lines.

Even if there are more than three vertical lines, draw the horizontal line first.

c) In the case of a horizontal, horizontal and vertical sequence:

Draw the two horizontal lines before the vertical lines.

Even in the case where other strokes are added, the horizontal lines are drawn first.

Even when there are more than three horizontal lines, this rule applies.

Even if the lines cross and the vertical line is curved, the horizontal line is drawn first.

d) In the case of a horizontal, horizontal, vertical, vertical line sequence:

The horizontal set of lines are drawn before the vertical set.

The second minor principle: These are basically concerned with exceptions to *the first minor principle,* that is, when the horizontal stroke proceeds the vertical. These exceptions include:

a) 田

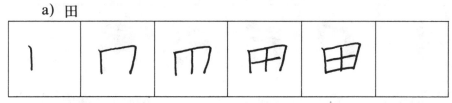

b) When a stroke or strokes extend from the basic form of a frame (□), the vertical line is drawn first.

Example:

c) 王

22

d) Variation of (c) 王

Even when one horizontal stroke is added to the basic form, the vertical line is drawn first.

As shown in (b), when a stroke or strokes extend from the basic form, the vertical line(s) are drawn first.

Examples:

Even in the case where one vertical stroke is added to the basic form, this rule applies.

The third minor principle:

The middle line is drawn first.

In the case where there is a line between one or two right-hand and left-hand strokes, the central line is drawn first.

Even when there are two lines between strokes on the left and right sides, the middle lines are drawn first.

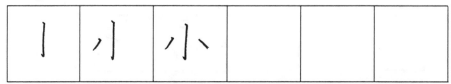

Even if the form becomes more complex, the central line is drawn first.

The two exceptions to this rule are:

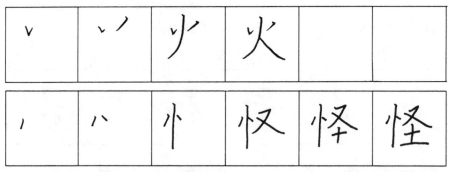

The fourth minor principle:

The enclosure is drawn first. When the basic form of the *kanji* is encased by outer strokes, the strokes of the frame are drawn first.

Examples:

Hi (日) and *Getsu* (月) are considered to be included in this category.

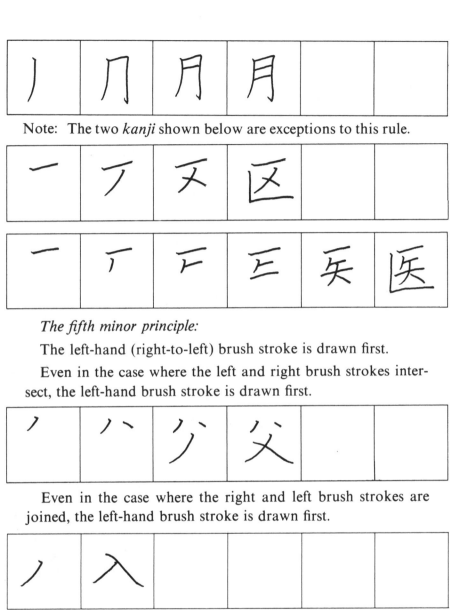

Note: The two *kanji* shown below are exceptions to this rule.

The fifth minor principle:

The left-hand (right-to-left) brush stroke is drawn first.

Even in the case where the left and right brush strokes intersect, the left-hand brush stroke is drawn first.

Even in the case where the right and left brush strokes are joined, the left-hand brush stroke is drawn first.

The sixth minor principle:

The vertical stroke is drawn last, slicing through the center of the character.

Even when the bottom point of the line is stopped by a horizontal stroke, the vertical stroke is drawn last.

Even when the top point of the line is stopped by a horizontal stroke, the vertical stroke is drawn last.

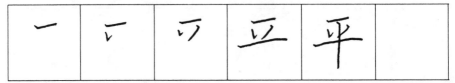

In the case where a tapering perpendicular line is stopped at each end by a horizontal line, the upper section of the *kanji* is drawn first, followed by the perpendicular line, and finished off by drawing the lower section of the *kanji*.

Please note the difference between the stroke orders of the following *kanji*.

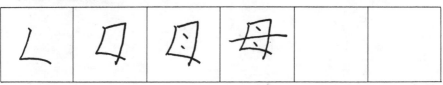

The seventh minor principle:

The horizontal stroke is drawn last, slicing through the center of the character.

Please take note of the exception to this rule.

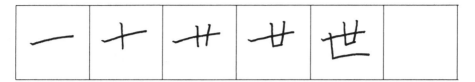

The eighth minor principle:

When the horizontal line is long and the left-hand brush stroke is short, the left-hand brush stroke is drawn first.

When the horizontal line is short and the left-hand brush stroke is long, the horizontal line is drawn first.

Examples:

a) When the left-hand stroke is drawn first:

b) When the horizontal line is drawn first.

Note: When drawing *kanji*, one should always pay attention to keeping the characters the same size.

Important Stroke Orders

(A) The following basic characters are those used in our daily writing. They are written with two or more kinds of stroke orders. To avoid confusing beginners, the stroke orders of characters shown in this book are only those that are most commonly used.

止	*SHI* *to(maru)*	stop	— ├ ├ 止 止 止 止 止 止 止	正 足 走 武
上	*JO* *ue*	up	— ├ 上 上 上 上 上 上 上 上	点 店
耳	*JI* *mimi*	ear	⌐ 厂 斤 斤 耳 耳 耳 耳 耳 耳	耳 *ear*
取	*SHU* *to(ru)*	take	⌐ 厂 斤 斤 耳 耳 取 取	最 職 厳
必	*HITSU* *kanara(zu)*	necessary always	ヽ ノ 必 必 必	
発	*HATSU* *HOTSU* *hana(tsu)*	departure a shot fire, shoot	ノ ヲ ヺ 欠 癶 癶 癶 癶 発	登

祭	SAI matsuri	fair festival	⁄	⁊	⁊	⁊	⁊⁷	
			夗	终	癸	祭	祭	
感	KAN	feeling emotion	)	厂	𠂉	后	咸	
			咸	咸	感	感	感	
盛	SEI sakari	peak summit	)	厂	万	成	成	
			成	成	盛	盛	盛	
馬	BA uma	horse	l	厂	丌	厈	㐅	
			馬	馬	馬	馬	馬	
唯	YUI tada	only	`	冂	口	口ʹ	叮	
			叮	吖	呼	唯	唯	
無	MU na(i)	without	⁄	𠂉	二	午	无	
			舞	無	無	無	無	
興	KOU oko(su)	revive	⌈	ʄ	阴	用	阋	
			阋	阋7	阋ʭ	鬪	興	

(B) Several *kanji* characters have no stroke orders, according to the rules. There are two *Nyo* groups of radicals. One group is written before the other sections of a character, and the other group is written last.

Note: A radical is a part of a *kanji* character used to arrange similar characters in a group.

29

a)

(1) *Nyo* radicals written first

   sui-nyo

処処	SHO *tokoro*	place	ノ　ク　タ　処　処

   sō-nyo

起	KI *o(kiru)*	get up	一　十　土　キ　キ 走　走　起　起　起

(2) *Nyo* radicals written last

   shin-nyo

近	KIN *chikai*	near	ノ　イ　ド　斤　斤 沂　近

	en-nyo

建	KEN, KON ta(teru)	build	ㄱ	ㄱ	ㅋ	ㅋ	ㅋ
			聿	律	建		

直	CHOKU tada(chi ni), naosu	at once, mend	一	十	亡	古	直
			直	直	直		

Note: As shown in the samples above, the radicals that take a position from the left side through the bottom of the character are called the *Nyo* or *Nyu* group.

b)

(1) Left sweeping written first

九	KYU kokono(tsu)	nine	ノ	九				及

(2) Left sweeping written last

力	RIKI chikara	power	ㄱ	力				刀 万 方 別

Chapter 1

The Japanese wrote *kanji* and *kana* (*hiragana* and *katakana*) with a brush before pens were imported from European countries at the beginning of the Meiji-era (1868-1912).

Writing by brush as an art form is called *Shodō* (calligraphy), and the writing for practical and daily use by ink pen is called *Pen-shūji* (penmanship).

At present, we write using ball-point pens, fountain pens, felt pens and pencils. Ink pens are now only used when students are practicing their penmanship in a copy book. However, delicate distinctions in the details of the strokes of each character can only be achieved by using a brush.

This book is written as an aid to learning practical penmanship, but not *Shodō* (calligraphy). However, we have added model hand-writing samples as an aid to understanding the details of the characters as written by brush. This should enable the reader to write even the most complicated of characters.

Various Handwriting Styles of *Kanji* and *Kana*

There are three accepted writing styles of *kanji* and *kana*.

    1. *kaisho* (print style)
    2. *gyōsho* (cursive style)
    3. *sōsho* (elaborate cursive style)

Japanese usually write in *gyōsho*, which is a simplified version of the printed style *kaisho*. However, as a beginner it is the *kaisho* style which must be studied first. Although this style is intricate, its intricacy is by far an easier means by which to study, learn, and remember *kanji*, in comparison to the abbreviated *gyōsho* style.

I would also recommend the enthusiastic student obtain a copy of a model handwriting book for Japanese students. These are not so expensive and provide clear detail of each *kanji* character.

How to Practice Writing *Kanji*

1. Each page introduces five *kanji* characters with similar characteristics.

   To show the parts of each character and the character's overall stroke order, we place the most basic character of each group in a large frame at the left of the top line of frames. This character is written with a brush, and provided with numbers indicating stroke order. The name of each of these basic characters, called radicals, appears to the lower right of the large frames.

2. Stroke orders for other characters are shown stroke-by-stroke at the lower left of each line of frames.

3. To the lower right of each line of frames are the character's *on*-reading (in italicized capital letters) and *kun*-reading (in italicized lower case letters). The number of strokes in the character is in parenthesis at the far right, and the character's meaning follows the *kun*-reading.

4. For practice, trace over the dotted lines and complete each character according to the stroke order to the lower left of the frames.

5. Every six pages you can practice exercises with compounds made from characters you learned on the previous pages.

1. "People" group characters

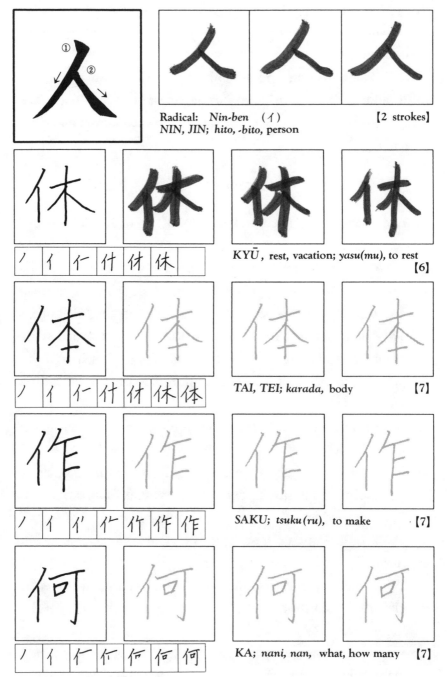

Radical: *Nin-ben* （亻） [2 strokes]
NIN, JIN; *hito, -bito,* person

ノ 亻 イ 什 付 休

KYŪ, rest, vacation; *yasu(mu),* to rest
【6】

ノ 亻 イ 什 付 休 体

TAI, TEI; *karada,* body 【7】

ノ 亻 イ′ 作 作 作 作

SAKU; *tsuku(ru),* to make 【7】

ノ 亻 イ 仁 仔 仔 何

KA; *nani, nan,* what, how many 【7】

34

2. "Tree" group characters

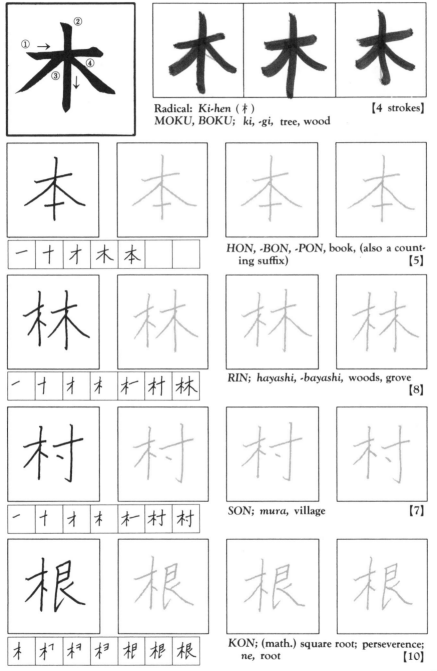

Radical: *Ki·hen* (木)　　　　　　　　**[4 strokes]**
MOKU, BOKU; *ki, -gi,* tree, wood

一　十　才　木　本

HON, -BON, -PON, book, (also a counting suffix)　　　　**[5]**

一　十　才　木　朾　村　林

RIN; *hayashi, -bayashi,* woods, grove
　　　　　　　　　　　　　　　　[8]

一　十　才　木　朾　村　村

SON; *mura,* village　　　　　　　**[7]**

木　朾　杓　杓　柑　根　根

KON; (math.) square root; perseverence; *ne,* root　　　　　　**[10]**

3. "Day" group characters

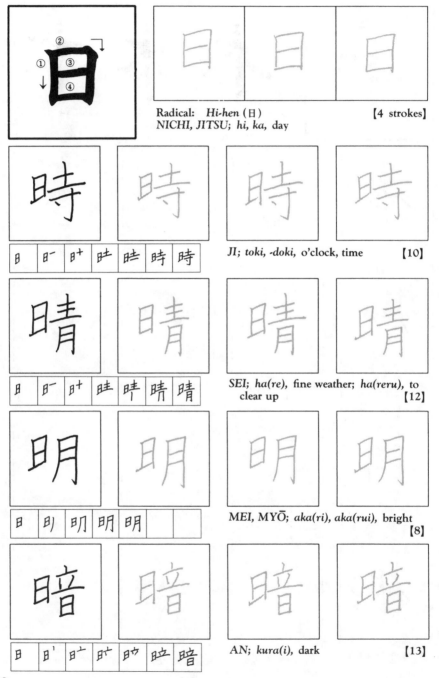

Radical: *Hi-hen* (日)   【4 strokes】
NICHI, JITSU; hi, ka, day

| 日 | 日⁻ | 日⁺ | 旷 | 眡 | 時 | 時 |

JI; toki, -doki, o'clock, time   【10】

| 日 | 日⁻ | 日⁺ | 旷 | 昡 | 晴 | 晴 |

SEI; ha(re), fine weather; *ha(reru)*, to
    clear up   【12】

| 日 | 日) | 明 | 明 | 明 | | |

MEI, MYŌ; aka(ri), aka(rui), bright
                    【8】

| 日 | 日' | 日⁻ | 日⁺ | 日亠 | 昡 | 暗 |

AN; kura(i), dark   【13】

4. "Sweeping stroke" group characters

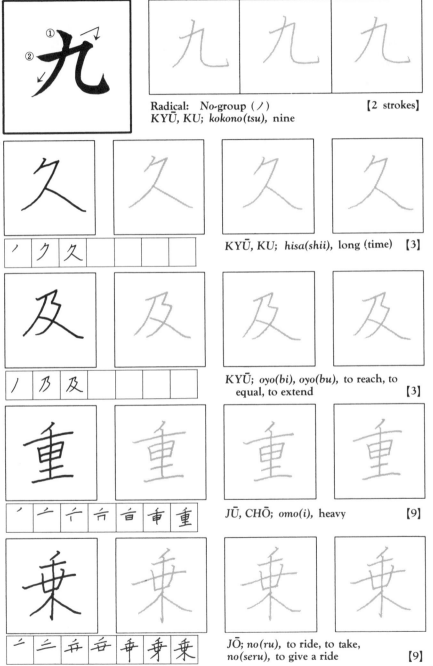

Radical: No-group (ノ) [2 strokes]
KYŪ, KU; kokono(tsu), nine

ノ ク 久

KYŪ, KU; hisa(shii), long (time) [3]

ノ 乃 及

KYŪ; oyo(bi), oyo(bu), to reach, to
equal, to extend [3]

ノ 一 一 一 一 一 重

JŪ, CHŌ; omo(i), heavy [9]

一 二 千 舌 垂 垂 乗

JŌ; no(ru), to ride, to take,
no(seru), to give a ride [9]

5. "Pot lid" group characters

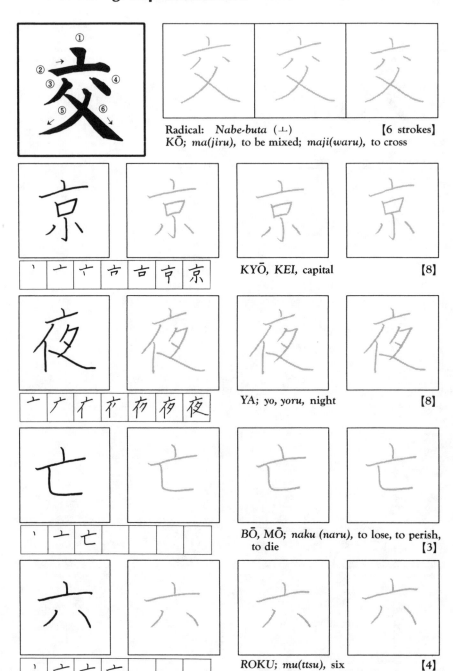

Radical: *Nabe-buta* (亠)   [6 strokes]
KŌ; *ma(jiru)*, to be mixed; *maji(waru)*, to cross

KYŌ, KEI, capital   [8]

YA; *yo, yoru*, night   [8]

BŌ, MŌ; *naku (naru)*, to lose, to perish,
    to die   [3]

ROKU; *mu(ttsu)*, six   [4]

6. "Grass crown" group characters

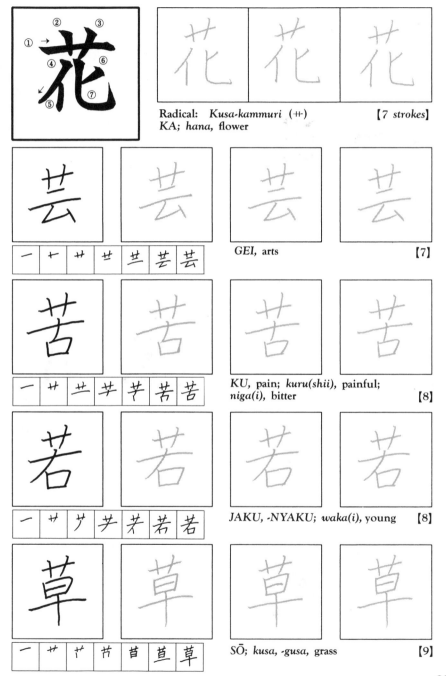

Radical: *Kusa-kammuri* (艹) 【7 strokes】
KA; *hana*, flower

GEI, arts 【7】

KU, pain; *kuru(shii)*, painful;
niga(i), bitter 【8】

JAKU, -NYAKU; *waka(i)*, young 【8】

SŌ; *kusa*, *-gusa*, grass 【9】

Exercise 1

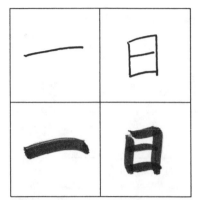

ichijitsu   1st day of the month;
ichinichi   one day

ni-hon   two long items

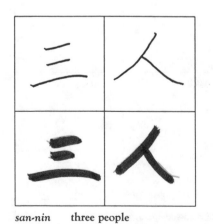

san-nin   three people

yo-sara   four dishes

go-gatsu   May

roku-mai   six pieces of (paper)

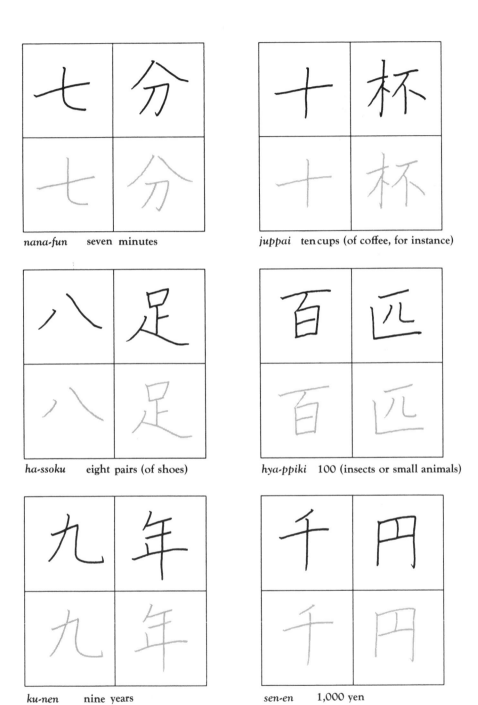

nana-fun   seven minutes

juppai   ten cups (of coffee, for instance)

ha-ssoku   eight pairs (of shoes)

hya-ppiki   100 (insects or small animals)

ku-nen   nine years

sen-en   1,000 yen

41

7. "Water" group characters

Radical: *Sanzui* (氵)
CHI; *ike*, pond, lake　　　　　[6 strokes]

KATSU, energy, liveliness　　　[9]

KAI; *umi*, sea, ocean　　　[9]

EI; *oyo(gu)*, to swim　　　[8]

KETSU; *ki(maru)*, to be decided;
ki(meru), to decide　　　[7]

8. "Roof" group characters

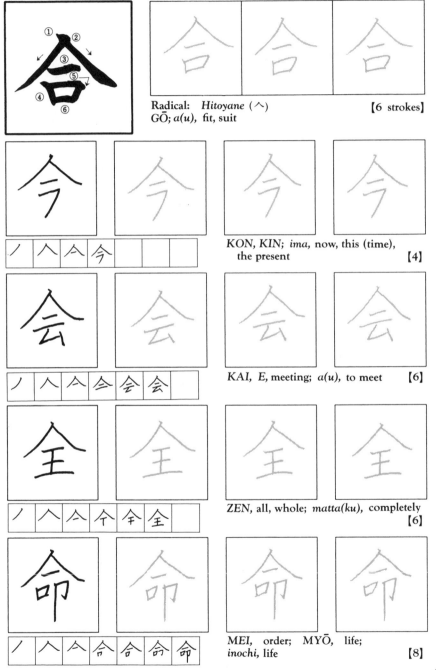

Radical: *Hitoyane* (へ)   [6 strokes]
GŌ; *a(u)*, fit, suit

KON, KIN; *ima*, now, this (time),
the present   [4]

KAI, E, meeting; *a(u)*, to meet   [6]

ZEN, all, whole; *matta(ku)*, completely
                                  [6]

MEI, order;   MYŌ, life;
inochi, life   [8]

9. "Tree with pent roof" group characters

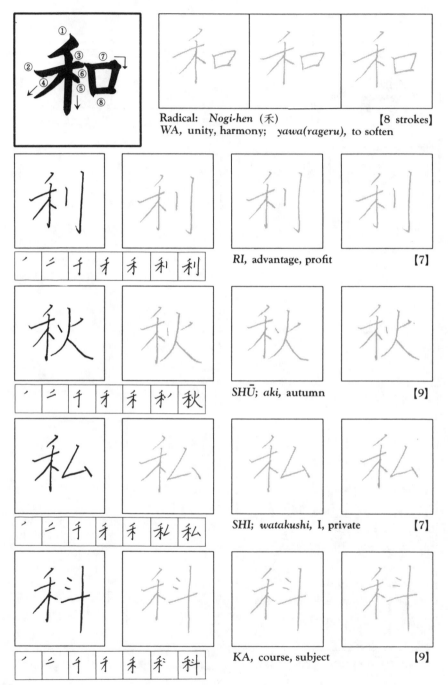

Radical: *Nogi-hen* (禾)　　　　　　　　　　【8 strokes】
WA, unity, harmony;　*yawa(rageru)*, to soften

RI, advantage, profit　　　　　　　　　　【7】

SHŪ; *aki*, autumn　　　　　　　　　　【9】

SHI; *watakushi*, I, private　　　　　　　【7】

KA, course, subject　　　　　　　　　　【9】

10. "Speak" group characters

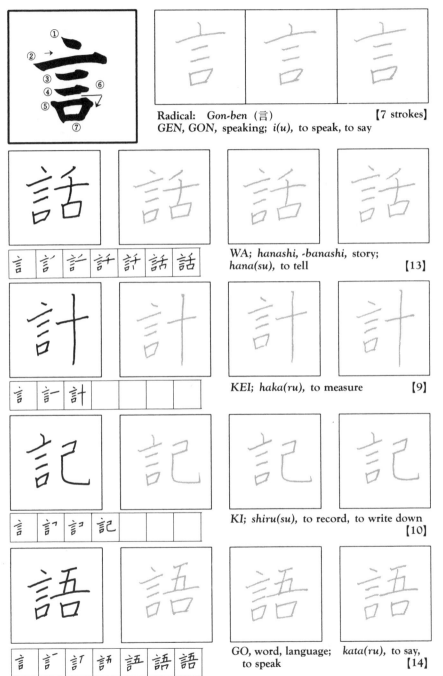

Radical: *Gon-ben* (言)　　　　　　　　　[7 strokes]
GEN, GON, speaking; *i(u)*, to speak, to say

WA; *hanashi*, -*banashi*, story;
hana(su), to tell　　　　　　　　　[13]

KEI; *haka(ru)*, to measure　　　　　[9]

KI; *shiru(su)*, to record, to write down
　　　　　　　　　　　　　　　　　[10]

GO, word, language;　*kata(ru)*, to say,
　to speak　　　　　　　　　　　　[14]

45

11. "Ground" group characters

Radical: *Tsuchi-hen* (土) 　　　　　　　　　　【3 strokes】
DO, TO; *tsuchi,* earth, ground

JŌ; *shiro,* castle 　　　　　　　　　　　　【9】

HAN; *saka, -zaka,* slope 　　　　　　　　　【7】

CHI, JI, earth, ground 　　　　　　　　　　【6】

JŌ; *ba,* place 　　　　　　　　　　　　　　【12】

12. "Frame" group characters

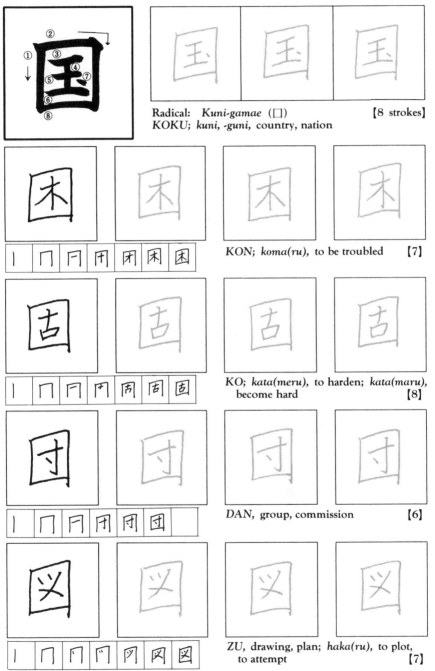

Radical: *Kuni-gamae* (口)   [8 strokes]
KOKU; *kuni, -guni,* country, nation

KON; *koma(ru),* to be troubled   [7]

KO; *kata(meru),* to harden; *kata(maru),*
  become hard   [8]

DAN, group, commission   [6]

ZU, drawing, plan; *haka(ru),* to plot,
  to attempt   [7]

Exercise 2

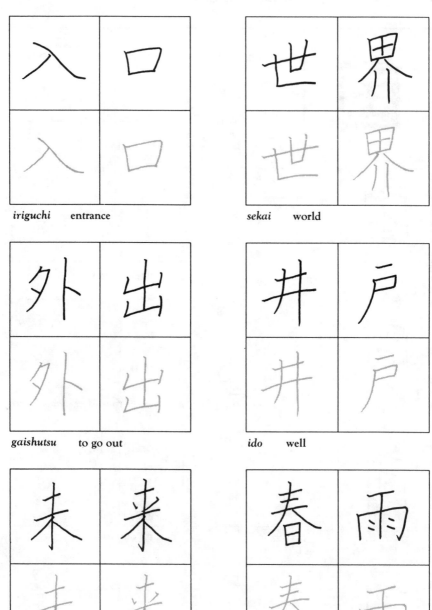

iriguchi entrance

sekai world

gaishutsu to go out

ido well

mirai future

harusame spring shower

48

shinrin   forest

fubo   parents

isha   doctor

kusabana   flower

kasen   river

heiya   plain

13. "Wide house" group characters

Radical: *Ma-dare* (广)　　　　　　　　【5 strokes】
KŌ; *hiro(i)*, wide; *hiro(-garu)*, to spread

KO, warehouse　　　　　【10】

TEN; *mise*, shop, store　　　　　【8】

TEI; *niwa*, garden　　　　　【10】

DO, -TO, TAKU; *tabi*, degree, time(s)
【9】

14. "Thread" group characters

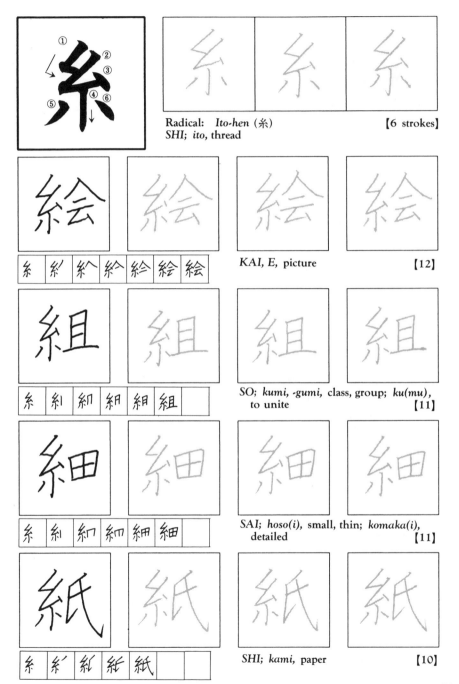

Radical: *Ito-hen* (糸) 【6 strokes】
SHI; *ito*, thread

KAI, E, picture 【12】

SO; *kumi, -gumi*, class, group; *ku(mu)*, to unite 【11】

SAI; *hoso(i)*, small, thin; *komaka(i)*, detailed 【11】

SHI; *kami*, paper 【10】

15. "Advance" group characters

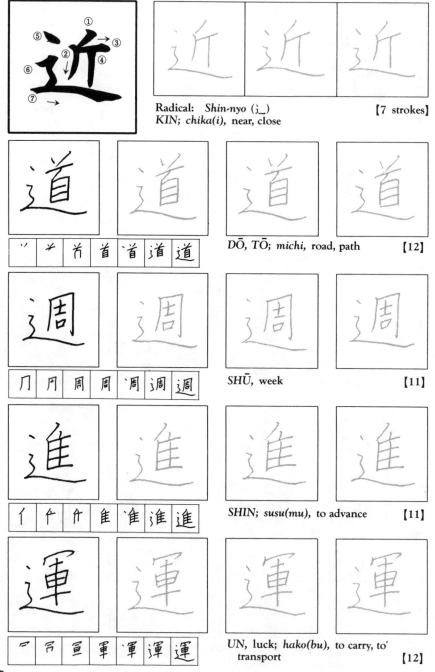

Radical: *Shin-nyo* (⻌)
KIN; *chika(i)*, near, close

【7 strokes】

DŌ, TŌ; *michi*, road, path 【12】

SHŪ, week 【11】

SHIN; *susu(mu)*, to advance 【11】

UN, luck; *hako(bu)*, to carry, to transport 【12】

16. "Door" group characters

Radical: *To-dare, To-kammuri* (戸) [4 strokes]
KO; *to, -do*, door, house

SHO, -JO; *tokoro, -dokoro*, place [8]

BŌ; *fusa*, chamber, house, cluster, tuft [8]

SEN; *ōgi*, folding fan [10]

HI; *tobira*, door [12]

53

17. "Scarecrow" group characters

Radical: *Haba* group (巾) 【5 strokes】
SHI, city; *ichi*, market

ノ ナ オ 右 布

FU, -PU; *nuno*, cloth 【5】

ノ メ ナ チ 斉 希 希

KI, rare, desire 【7】

l ⺌ ⺌ 岩 常 常 常

JŌ; *tsune*, usual, ordinary 【11】

巾 帜 帷 帳 帳 帳

CHŌ, curtain, notebook 【11】

18. "Heart" group characters

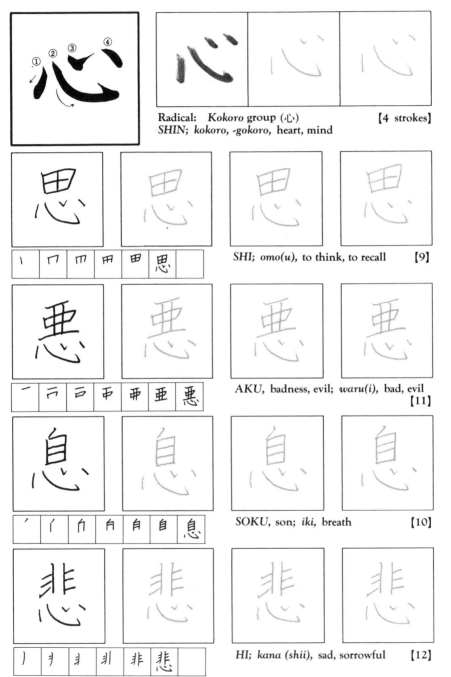

Radical: *Kokoro* group (心)   **[4 strokes]**
SHIN; *kokoro, -gokoro,* heart, mind

SHI; *omo(u)*, to think, to recall   **[9]**

AKU, badness, evil; *waru(i)*, bad, evil
         [11]

SOKU, son; *iki*, breath   **[10]**

HI; *kana (shii)*, sad, sorrowful   **[12]**

Exercise 3

komugi   wheat

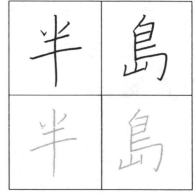

hantō   peninsula

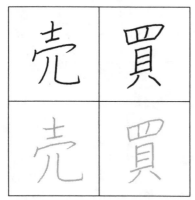

baibai   buying and selling

kaisha   company

読書

dokusho   reading

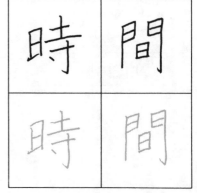

jikan   hour, time

shoka   early summer

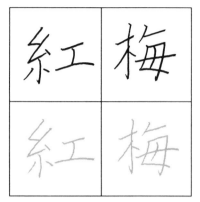

kōbai   Japanese apricot with red blossoms

banshū   late autumn

gakkō   school

suidō   tap water

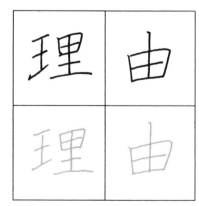

riyū   reason

19. "Fire" group characters

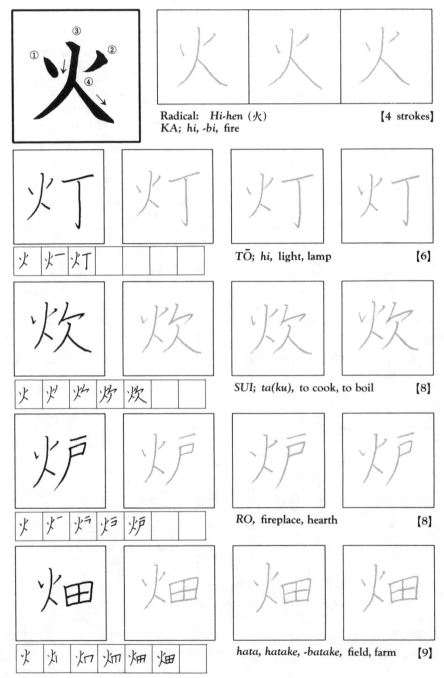

Radical: *Hi-hen* (火) 【4 strokes】
KA; *hi, -bi,* fire

TŌ; hi, light, lamp [6]

SUI; ta(ku), to cook, to boil [8]

RO, fireplace, hearth [8]

hata, hatake, -batake, field, farm [9]

20. "Flame" group characters

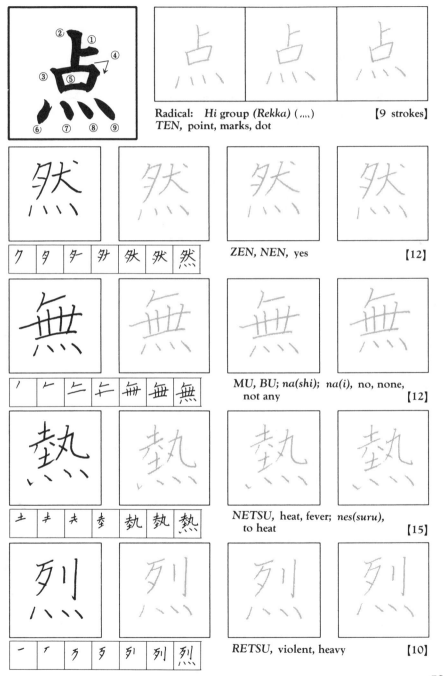

Radical: *Hi* group *(Rekka)* (….) **[9 strokes]**
TEN, point, marks, dot

ZEN, NEN, yes **[12]**

MU, BU; *na(shi)*; *na(i)*, no, none, not any **[12]**

NETSU, heat, fever; *nes(suru)*, to heat **[15]**

RETSU, violent, heavy **[10]**

21. "God" group characters

Radical: *Shimesu-hen* (礻) 　　　　　【7 strokes】
SHA, -JA, a firm; *yashiro*, shrine

SHIN, JIN; *kami*, god 　　　　　【9】

REI, courtesy, thanks, reward, to bow
　　　　　【5】

KI; *ino(ru)*, to pray 　　　　　【8】

FUKU; good fortune, good luck 　【13】

22. "Bow" group characters

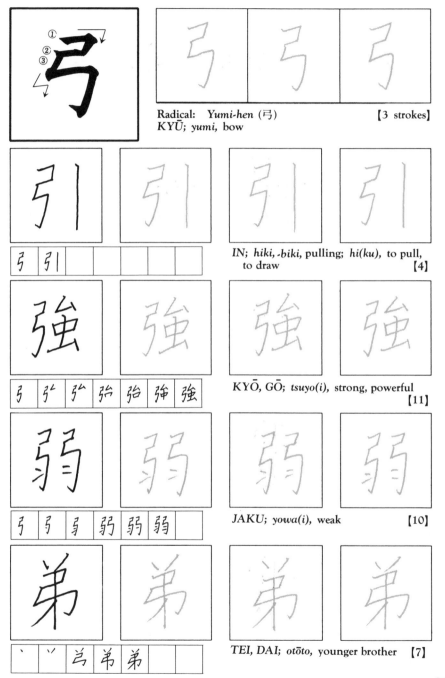

Radical: *Yumi-hen* (弓)　　　　　　【3 strokes】
KYŪ; *yumi,* bow

IN; *hiki, -biki,* pulling; *hi(ku),* to pull, to draw　　【4】

KYŌ, GŌ; *tsuyo(i),* strong, powerful 【11】

JAKU; *yowa(i),* weak　　　　　【10】

TEI, DAI; *otōto,* younger brother 【7】

23. "Rain" group characters

Radical: *Ame-kammuri* (⻗)   【8 strokes】
U; *ame,* rain

UN; *kumo,* cloud   【12】

SETSU; *yuki,* snow   【11】

DEN, electricity, lightning   【13】

RAI; *kaminari,* thunder, thunderbolt
    【13】

24. "Bamboo" group characters

Radical: *Tahe-kammuri* (ᙏ)   **[6 strokes]**
CHIKU; *take, -dake,* bamboo

TŌ, -DŌ; kota(e), kota(eru), (to) answer   **[12]**

TŌ, class, quality; *hito(shii),* equal   **[12]**

TEKI; fue, flute   **[11]**

hako, -bako, box, case   **[15]**

Exercise 4

kyōdai   brother

chikurin   bamboo grove

jinja (Shinto)   shrine

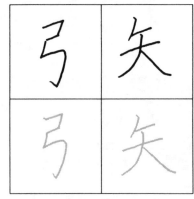

yumiya   bow and arrow

raiun   thunder cloud

tenka　ignition

tōzen　naturally

kyōjaku　strength

tahata　fields

nesshin　zeal

tōdai　lighthouse

25. "Ax" group characters

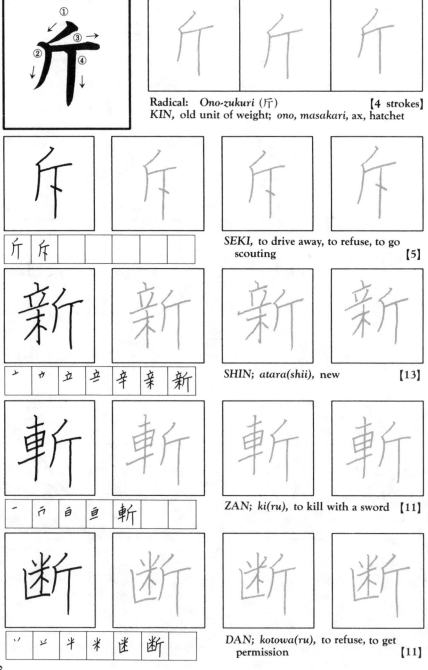

Radical: *Ono-zukuri* (斤)　　　　　　　[4 strokes]
KIN, old unit of weight; *ono, masakari*, ax, hatchet

SEKI, to drive away, to refuse, to go scouting　　[5]

SHIN; *atara(shii)*, new　　[13]

ZAN; *ki(ru)*, to kill with a sword　[11]

DAN; *kotowa(ru)*, to refuse, to get permission　　[11]

26. "Wa on the top" group characters

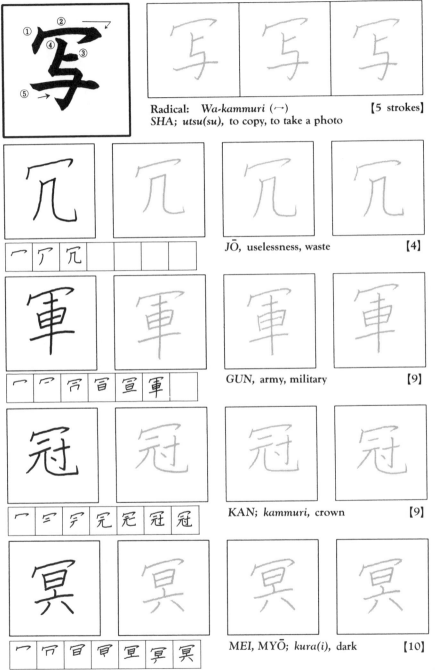

Radical: *Wa-kammuri* (⌐) 【5 strokes】
SHA; *utsu(su)*, to copy, to take a photo

JŌ, uselessness, waste 【4】

GUN, army, military 【9】

KAN; *kammuri*, crown 【9】

MEI, MYŌ; *kura(i)*, dark 【10】

27. "*Sun*" group characters

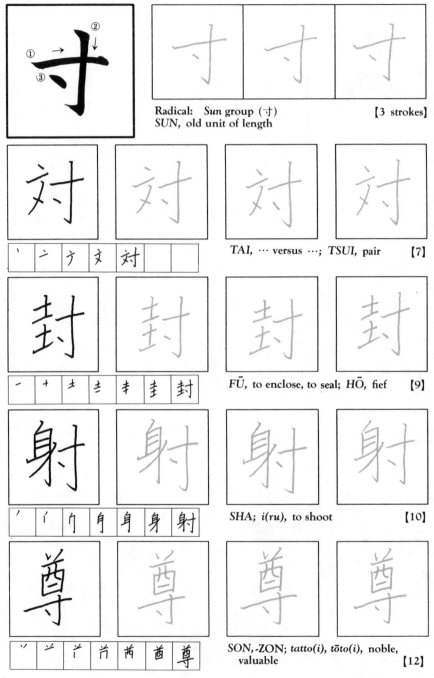

Radical: *Sun* group (寸)
SUN, old unit of length

【3 strokes】

TAI, ··· versus ···; TSUI, pair 【7】

FŪ, to enclose, to seal; HŌ, fief 【9】

SHA; i(ru), to shoot 【10】

SON, -ZON; tatto(i), tōto(i), noble,
valuable 【12】

28. "Stand" group characters

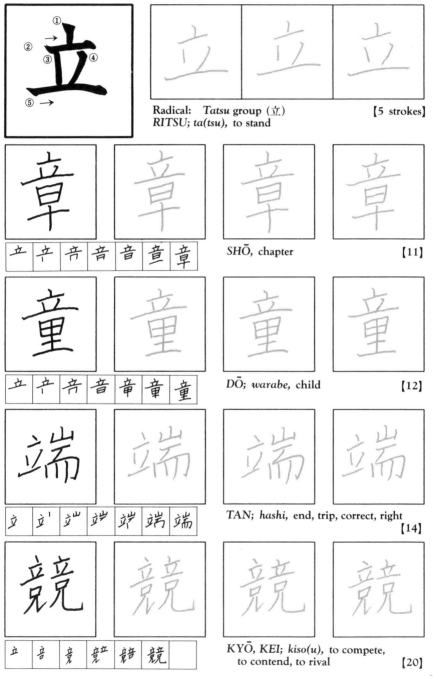

Radical: *Tatsu* group (立)   [5 strokes]
RITSU; *ta(tsu)*, to stand

SHŌ, chapter   [11]

DŌ; *warabe*, child   [12]

TAN; *hashi*, end, trip, correct, right
                                               [14]

KYŌ, KEI; *kiso(u)*, to compete,
to contend, to rival   [20]

69

29. "Town" group characters

Radical: Ōzato group (阝)   【11 strokes】
BU, department, part, copy

一 十 土 耂 耂 者 者 都

TO, TSU; miyako, capital   【11】

一 二 三 丯 邦

HŌ, country, land   【7】

一 匚 牙 牙 邪

JA, evil, wicked   【7】

丶 亠 亠 六 亣 交 郊

KŌ, suburbs, country   【9】

30. "Sickness" group characters

Radical: *Yamai-dare* (疒)   【10 strokes】
BYŌ; *yamai*, illness; *ya(mu)*, to fall ill

TSŪ; *ita(mi)*, pain; *ita(mu)*, to have
   a pain, to ache   【12】

HI; *tsuka(re)*, fatigue; *tsuka(reru)*,
   to get tired   【10】

EKI, epidemic   【9】

SHITSU, sickness   【10】

Exercise 5

toshi   city

hirō   fatigue

kōgai   suburb

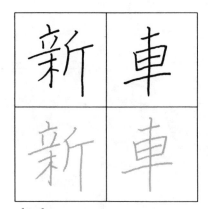

shinsha   new car

jaaku   evil

hassha   shooting

jōdan　joke

sonkei　respect

hōgaku　Japanese music

haiseki　rejection

dangen　declaration

jidō　child

31. "Sheep" group characters

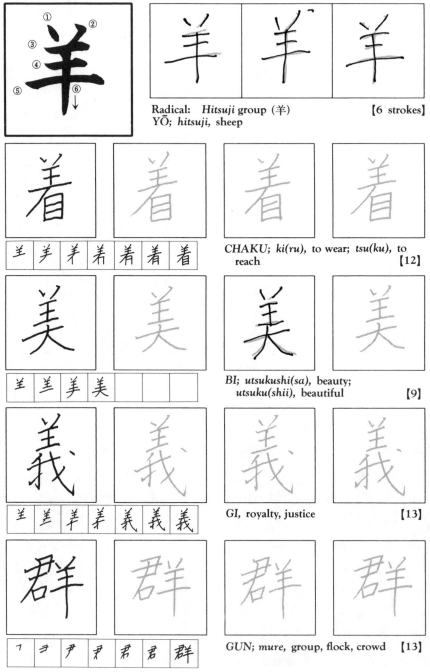

Radical: *Hitsuji* group (羊) 【6 strokes】
YŌ; *hitsuji,* sheep

CHAKU; *ki(ru),* to wear; *tsu(ku),* to reach 【12】

BI; *utsukushi(sa),* beauty; *utsuku(shii),* beautiful 【9】

GI, royalty, justice 【13】

GUN; *mure,* group, flock, crowd 【13】

32. "Bird" group characters

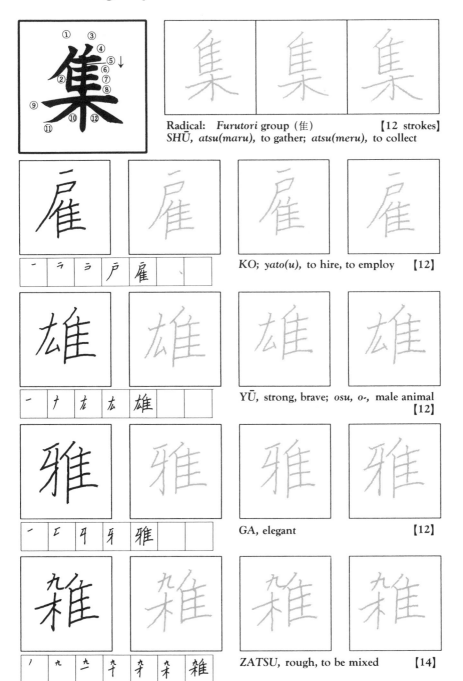

Radical: *Furutori* group (隹) 【12 strokes】
SHŪ, *atsu(maru)*, to gather; *atsu(meru)*, to collect

ー ラ ヲ 戸 雇 ヽ

KO; *yato(u)*, to hire, to employ 【12】

ー ナ ナ 左 雄

YŪ, strong, brave; *osu, o-*, male animal 【12】

ー エ 牙 牙 雅

GA, elegant 【12】

丿 九 九 杂 杂 杂 雑

ZATSU, rough, to be mixed 【14】

33. "Chicken" group characters

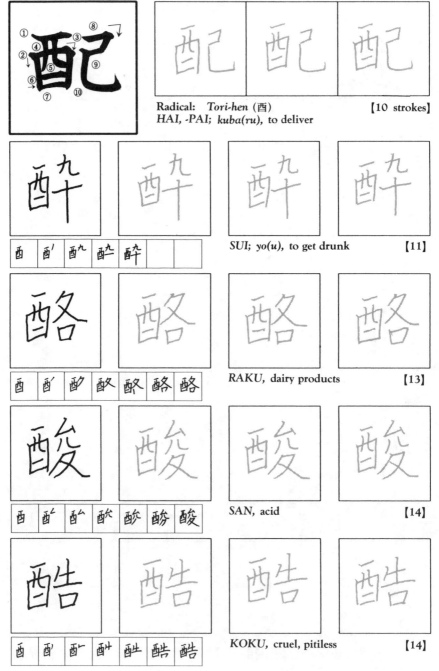

Radical: *Tori-hen* (酉) [10 strokes]
HAI, -PAI; *kuba(ru)*, to deliver

SUI; *yo(u)*, to get drunk 【11】

RAKU, dairy products 【13】

SAN, acid 【14】

KOKU, cruel, pitiless 【14】

34. "Mouth" group characters

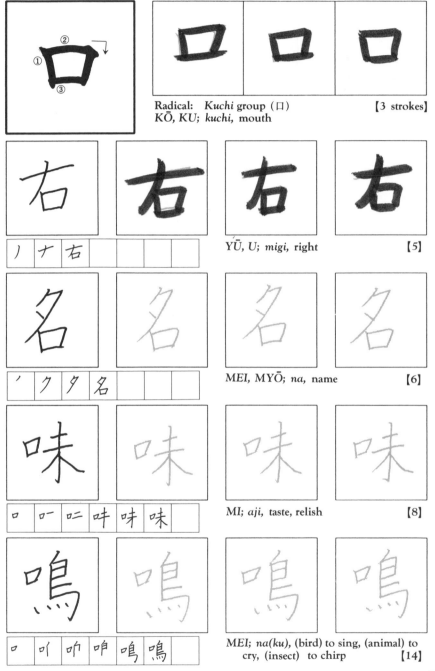

Radical: *Kuchi* group (口) [3 strokes]
KŌ, KU; *kuchi,* mouth

ノ ナ 右

YŪ, U; *migi,* right 【5】

' ク タ 名

MEI, MYŌ; *na,* name 【6】

ロ ロー ロ二 叶 味 味

MI; *aji,* taste, relish 【8】

ロ 叮 叭 咟 鳴 鳴

MEI; *na(ku),* (bird) to sing, (animal) to cry, (insect) to chirp 【14】

77

35. "Walk" group characters

Radical: *Gyōnin-ben* (彳) 【8 strokes】
Ō; *yu(ku)*, to go

YAKU, duty, role; EKI, (lit.) war 【7】

HI; *kare*, he 【8】

TAI; *ma(tsu)*, to wait for 【9】

GO, KŌ; *ushi(ro)*, behind; *nochi*, after 【9】

78

36. "Animal" group characters

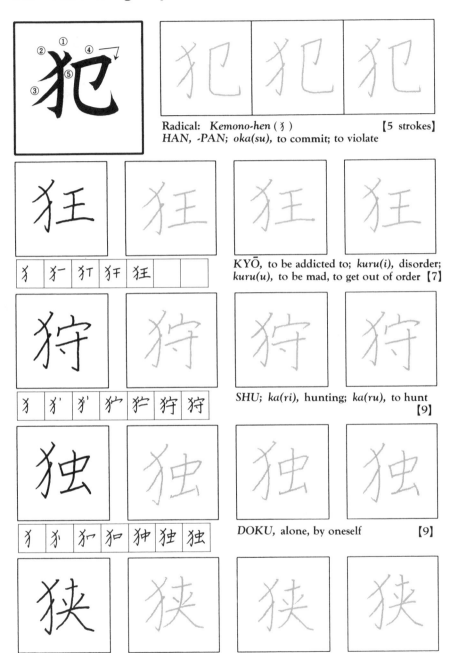

Radical: *Kemono-hen* (犭) [5 strokes]
HAN, -PAN; *oka(su)*, to commit; to violate

KYŌ, to be addicted to; *kuru(i)*, disorder;
kuru(u), to be mad, to get out of order 【7】

SHU; *ka(ri)*, hunting; *ka(ru)*, to hunt
【9】

DOKU, alone, by oneself 【9】

KYŌ; *sema(i)*, narrow, small 【9】

Exercise 6

bimi   delicious

zasshi   magazine

dokusen   monopoly

guntō   group of islands

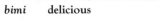

shūhai   collection and delivery

kyōshō   narrow

往来　*ōrai*　traffic

役所　*yakusho*　public office

熱狂　*nekkyō*　enthusiasm

彼岸　*higan*　equinoctial week

犯人　*hannin*　criminal

午後　*gogo*　afternoon

37. "Mountain" group characters

Radical: *Yama* group (山)　　　【3 strokes】
SAN, -Zan; *yama*, mountain

GAN; *iwa*, rock　　　【8】

GAN; *kishi*, -*gishi*, bank, shore　　　【8】

TAN; *sumi*, charcoal　　　【9】

TŌ; *shima*, -*jima*, island　　　【10】

38. "Vehicle" group characters

Radical: *Kuruma-hen* (車)　　　　　　【7 strokes】
SHA; *kuruma,* vehicle

KEI; *karu, -garu, karu(i),* (weight)
　　light, slight, easy　　　　　　【12】

TEN; *koro(bu),* to roll, to fall, to change
　　　　　　　　　　　　　　　　【11】

RIN; *wa,* ring, circle, wheel　　　【15】

YU, transport, send　　　　　　　【16】

39. "Stone" group characters

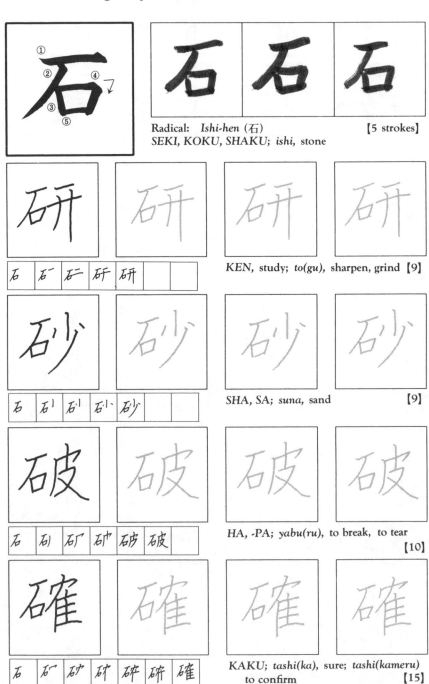

Radical: *Ishi-hen* (石) [5 strokes]
SEKI, KOKU, SHAKU; *ishi*, stone

KEN, study; *to(gu)*, sharpen, grind [9]

SHA, SA; *suna*, sand [9]

HA, -PA; *yabu(ru)*, to break, to tear [10]

KAKU; *tashi(ka)*, sure; *tashi(kameru)*
to confirm [15]

84

40. "Gate" group characters

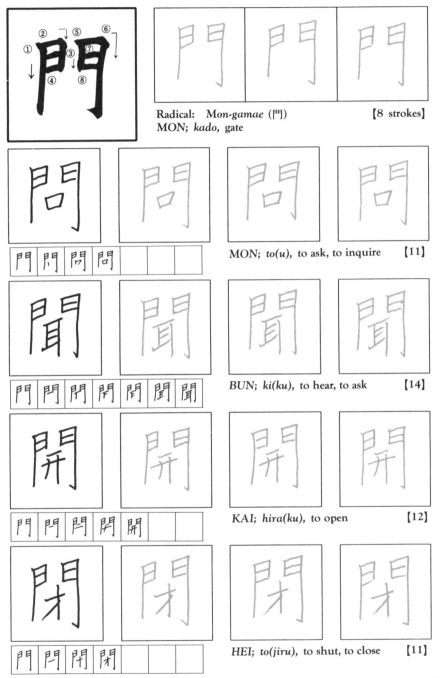

Radical: *Mon-gamae* (門)   [8 strokes]
MON; *kado*, gate

MON; *to(u)*, to ask, to inquire   [11]

BUN; *ki(ku)*, to hear, to ask   [14]

KAI; *hira(ku)*, to open   [12]

HEI; *to(jiru)*, to shut, to close   [11]

41. "*U* on the top" group characters

Radical: *U-kammuri* (⼧)   【6 strokes】
JI, letter; *aza*, a (village) section

AN, to feel easy; *yasu(i)*, cheap   [6]

KYAKU, -KAKU, guest   [9]

KYŪ, -GŪ, KU; *miya*, shrine,
    prince(-cess)   [10]

JITSU, truth; *mi*, nut, fruit; *mino(ru)*
    to bear fruit   [8]

42. "Child" group characters

Radical: Ko group (子)   【3 strokes】
SHI, SU; ko, -go, child

ZON, SON, to exist; zon(zuru),
to know, to think   【6】

GAKU, learning; mana(bu), to learn   【8】

KI, season   【8】

SON; mago, grandchild   【10】

Exercise 7

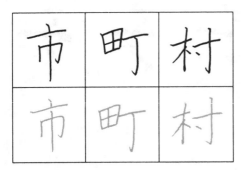

shi-chō-son
cities, towns, and villages

shison
descendant

nengappi
a date

zaigaku
attending school

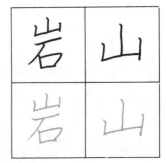

Tōkyō-to
Tokyo Metropolitan Area

iwayama
rocky mountain

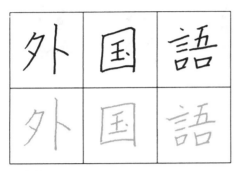

gaikokugo
foreign language

unten
drive

kyōkasho
textbook

hamon
expulsion

kuyakusho
ward office

genjitsu
actuality

43. "Moon" group characters

Radical: *Tsuki* group   〔4 strokes〕
GETSU, -GATSU; *tsuki, -zuki,* moon, month

CHŌ; *asa,* morning   【12】

KI, -GO, period, term   【12】

SHŌ; *katsu,* to win   【12】

FUKU, dress, Western clothes   【8】

44. "King" group characters

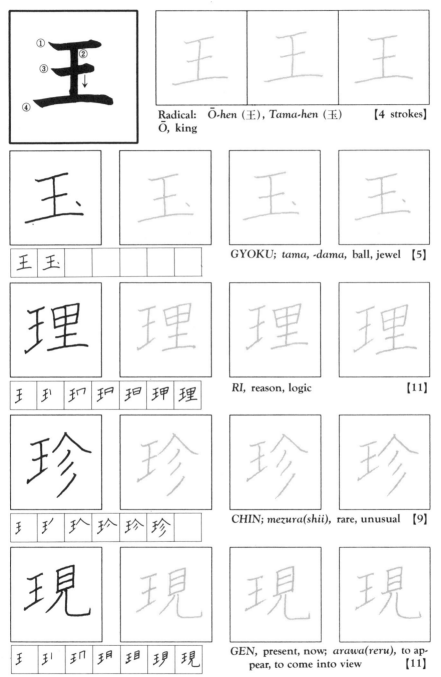

Radical: Ō-hen (王), *Tama-hen* (王) [4 strokes]
Ō, king

GYOKU; *tama, -dama,* ball, jewel [5]

RI, reason, logic [11]

CHIN; *mezura(shii),* rare, unusual [9]

GEN, present, now; *arawa(reru),* to appear, to come into view [11]

45. "Hole" group characters

Radical: Ana-kammuri (穴) 【5 strokes】
KETSU; ana, hole, cave

KŪ; sora, -zora, sky 【8】

KYŪ, study 【7】

SŌ; mado, window 【11】

CHITSU, to block; nitrogen 【11】

46. "Look" group characters

Radical: *Miru* group (見) 　　　　　【7 strokes】
KEN; *mi(ru)*, to see, to look

KI, compass, rule, to measure 　　　【11】

KAKU; *obo(eru)*, to remember, to understand 　　　【12】

SHIN; *oya*, parent; *shita(shii)*, close, familiar 　　　【16】

KAN; observation, view, way of thinking 　　　【18】

47. "Ear" group characters

Radical: *Mimi-hen* (耳)   [6 strokes]
JI; mimi, ear

SHU; *to(ru),* to take, to get, to get hold of   [8]

CHI; *haji,* shame, disgrace; *hazu(kashii),* shameful, disgraceful   [10]

SHOKU, occupation, trade, vocation   [18]

CHŌ, listening   [17]

48. "Two feet" group characters

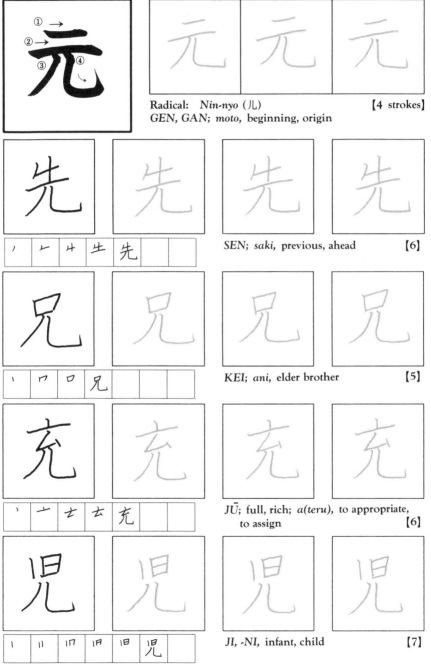

Radical: *Nin-nyo* (儿) 　　　　　　【4 strokes】
GEN, GAN; *moto,* beginning, origin

先　　　　　先　　　先

SEN; *saki,* previous, ahead 　　　　【6】

兄　　　　　兄　　　兄

KEI; *ani,* elder brother 　　　　　【5】

充　　　　　充　　　充

JŪ; full, rich; *a(teru),* to appropriate,
　　to assign 　　　　　　　　　　【6】

児　　　　　児　　　児

JI, -NI, infant, child 　　　　　　　【7】

Exercise 8

sankaku-kei
triangle

anzen
safety

chosuichi
reservoir

sūji
number

図書館

toshokan
library

chinkyaku
a guest visiting after
long absence

96

hokōsha
pedestrian

kigen
period

myōgonichi
the day after tomorrow

shōri
victory

新聞紙

shimbunshi
newspaper

temmado
skylight

49. "Gold (Metal)" group characters

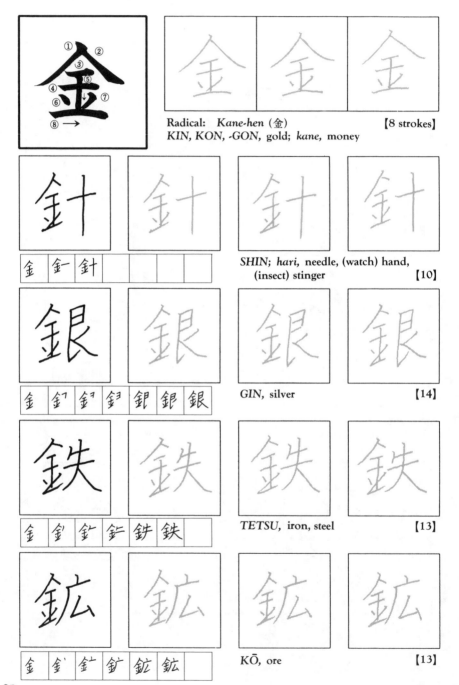

Radical: *Kane-hen* (金) 　　　　　　　【8 strokes】
KIN, KON, -GON, gold; *kane,* money

金 釒─針

SHIN; hari, needle, (watch) hand,
(insect) stinger 　　　　　　　　【10】

金 釒⁷ 釒ㄱ 釒ㇷ 鉅 銀 銀

GIN, silver 　　　　　　　　　　【14】

金 釒 釒─ 釒─ 鉄─ 鉄

TETSU, iron, steel 　　　　　　　【13】

金 釒` 釒─ 釒─ 鉱 鉱

KŌ, ore 　　　　　　　　　　　　【13】

50. "Woman" group characters

Radial: *Onna-hen* (女) 【3 strokes】
JO, NYO; *onna*, woman, girl

SHI; *ane*, elder sister [8]

MAI; *imōto*, younger sister [8]

SHI; *haji(maru)*, to begin [8]

KŌ; *kono(mu)*, *su(ki)*, to like, to love
[6]

51. "Hand" group characters

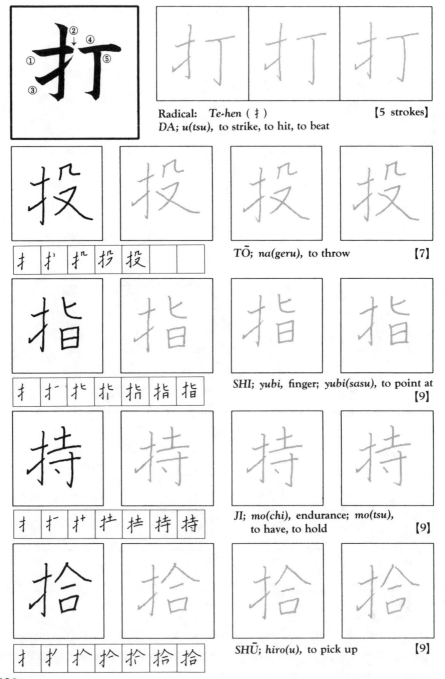

Radical: *Te-hen* (扌)　　　　　　　　**[5 strokes]**
DA; *u(tsu)*, to strike, to hit, to beat

TŌ; *na(geru)*, to throw　　　　　　　　【7】

SHI; *yubi*, finger; *yubi(sasu)*, to point at
【9】

JI; *mo(chi)*, endurance; *mo(tsu)*,
　to have, to hold　　　　　　　　【9】

SHŪ; *hiro(u)*, to pick up　　　　　　　【9】

52. "Roof and two crossed lines" group characters

Radical: *Boku-nyo* group (攵)　　　　　【7 strokes】
KŌ; *se(meru)*, to attack, to assault

KAI; *arata(meru)*, to change, to revise
【7】

HŌ; *hana(su)*, to let go, to release　【8】

KYŌ; *oshie(ru)*, to teach　　　　　【11】

SEI, SHŌ; *matsurigoto*, government 【9】

53. "Big shell" group characters

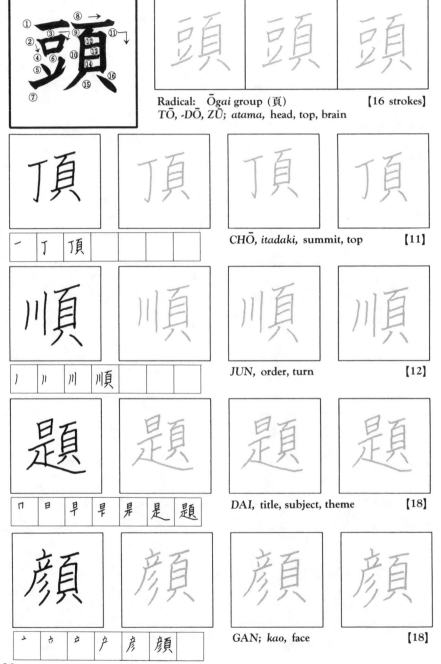

Radical: Ōgai group (頁)　　　　　　[16 strokes]
TŌ, -DŌ, ZŪ; *atama*, head, top, brain

一　丁　頂

CHŌ, *itadaki,* summit, top　　　[11]

丿　川　川　順

JUN, order, turn　　　[12]

冂　日　旦　早　早　是　題

DAI, title, subject, theme　　　[18]

亠　立　立　产　彦　顔

GAN; *kao,* face　　　[18]

54. "Feather" group characters

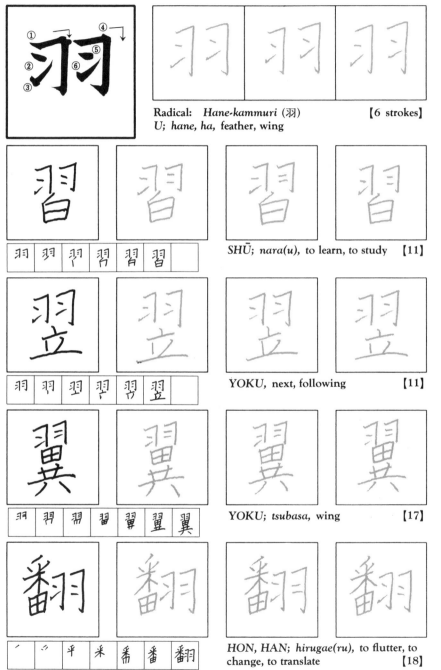

Radical: *Hane-kammuri* (羽)　　　　[6 strokes]
U; *hane, ha,* feather, wing

SHŪ; *nara(u)*, to learn, to study　　[11]

YOKU, next, following　　[11]

YOKU; *tsubasa*, wing　　[17]

HON, HAN; *hirugae(ru)*, to flutter, to change, to translate　　[18]

Exercise 9

shun-ka-shū-tō
the four seasons

tō-zai-nan-boku
all directions

kōtō-gakkō
high school

Tokyō Daigaku
Tokyo University

seimeihoken
life insurance

shochū-mimai
summer greeting card

Nihon rettō
the Japanese Islands

tairyō seisan
mass production

hoikuen-ji
children attending nursery school

Edo jidai
the Edo era

55. "Clothing" group characters

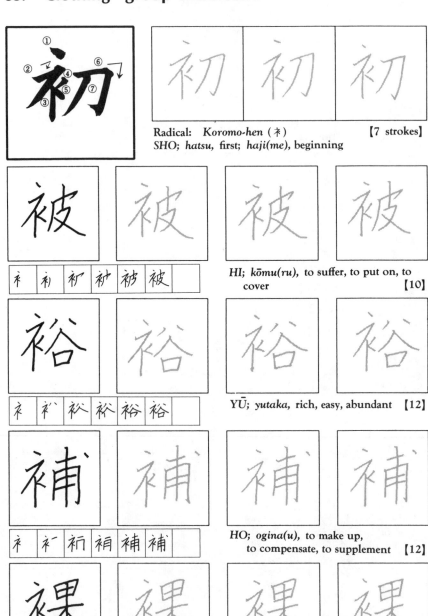

Radical: *Koromo-hen* (衤) 【7 strokes】
SHO; *hatsu*, first; *haji(me)*, beginning

HI; *kōmu(ru)*, to suffer, to put on, to
cover 【10】

YŪ; *yutaka*, rich, easy, abundant 【12】

HO; *ogina(u)*, to make up,
to compensate, to supplement 【12】

RA; *hadaka*, nude 【13】

56. "Small village" group characters

Radical: *Kozato-hen* (阝)　　　　【7 strokes】
BŌ; *fuse(gu)*, to defend, to prevent

IN, (Buddhist) temple, a board,
　　a house of government　　【10】

KŌ; *fu(ru)*, to fall (rain); *o(riru)*,
　　to get off　　【10】

YŌ, sun, cheerful, positive　　【12】

KAI, -GAI, floor, story (of a building)
　　【12】

107

57. "Food" group characters

Radical: *Shoku* group (食)   [9 strokes]
SHOKU, -JIKI, food; *ku(u)*, *ta(beru)*, to eat

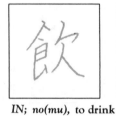

IN; *no(mu)*, to drink   【12】

| 食 | 飠 | 飲 | 飲 | 飲 | |

HAN, -PAN; *meshi*, cooked rice, meal
      【12】

| 食 | 飠 | 飣 | 飯 | 飯 | |

SHOKU; *kaza(ru)*, to decorate,
      to ornament   【13】

| 食 | 飠 | 飲 | 飣 | 飾 | 飾 | |

KAN; *yakata*, *tate*, building, hall,
      mansion   【16】

| 食 | 飠 | 飣 | 飣 | 館 | 館 | 館 |

58. "Robe" group characters

Radical: *Koromo* group (衣)   [6 strokes]
I; *koromo*, clothes, garment, priest's robe

ノ	イ	亻	代	代	袋

TAI; *fukuro*, bag, sack   [11]

一	十	夫	主	表	

HYŌ, -PYŌ, list, chart, table; *omote*, outside, surface; *ara(wasu)*, to show [8]

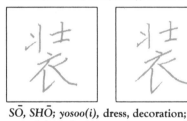

丨	丨	丬	丬丄	丬丄	壯	裝

SŌ, SHŌ; *yosoo(i)*, dress, decoration; *yosoo(u)*, to dress, to wear [12]

一	十	土	表	裁	裁	裁

SAI, to judge; *ta(tsu)*, to cut out (a dress)   [12]

59. "Rice field" group characters

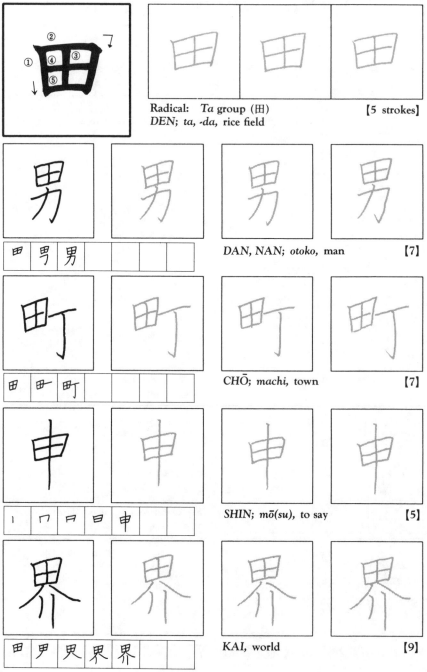

Radical: *Ta* group (田) 【5 strokes】
DEN; *ta, -da,* rice field

DAN, NAN; *otoko,* man 【7】

CHŌ; *machi,* town 【7】

SHIN; *mō(su),* to say 【5】

KAI, world 【9】

60. "Rice" group characters

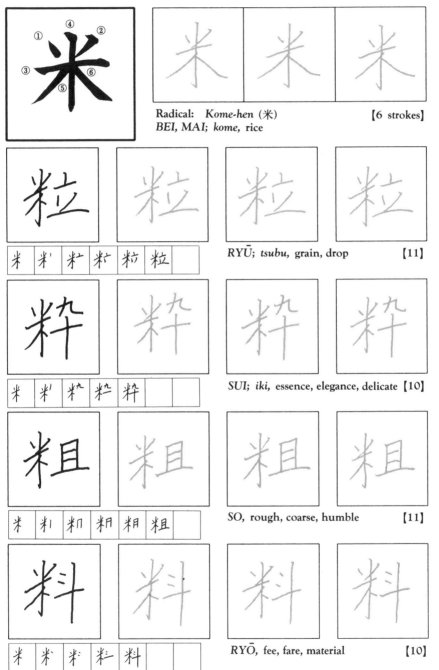

Radical: *Kome-hen* (米)   [6 strokes]
BEI, MAI; kome, rice

RYŪ; *tsubu,* grain, drop   [11]

SUI; *iki,* essence, elegance, delicate [10]

SO, rough, coarse, humble   [11]

RYŌ, fee, fare, material   [10]

Exercise 10

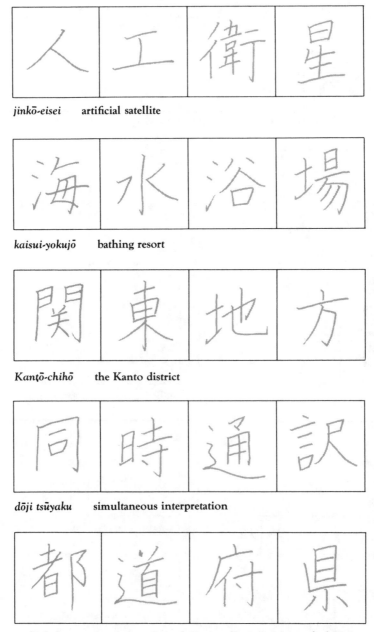

jinkō-eisei   artificial satellite

kaisui-yokujō   bathing resort

Kantō-chihō   the Kanto district

dōji tsūyaku   simultaneous interpretation

to-dō-fu-ken   the metropolis and districts (Japan's system of administrative government)

nen-jū-mukyū　　"Open throughout the Year"

Sōri-dajin　　the Prime Minister

Meiji-jingū　　Meiji Shrine

Fuji-sanchō　　the summit of Mt. Fuji

kabushiki-gaisha　　joint-stock company

61. "Direction" group characters

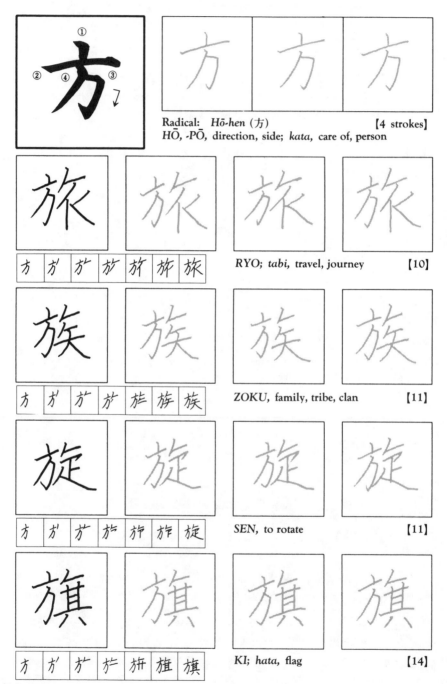

Radical: *Hō-hen* (方) 　　　　　　　　　【4 strokes】
HŌ, -PŌ, direction, side; *kata*, care of, person

方　方　が　扩　抃　旂　旅　　RYO; *tabi*, travel, journey　　【10】

方　が　扩　扩　斿　族　族　　ZOKU, family, tribe, clan　　【11】

方　が　扩　扩　抃　旂　旋　　SEN, to rotate　　【11】

方　が　扩　扩　拼　旆　旗　　KI; *hata*, flag　　【14】

62. "Eye" group characters

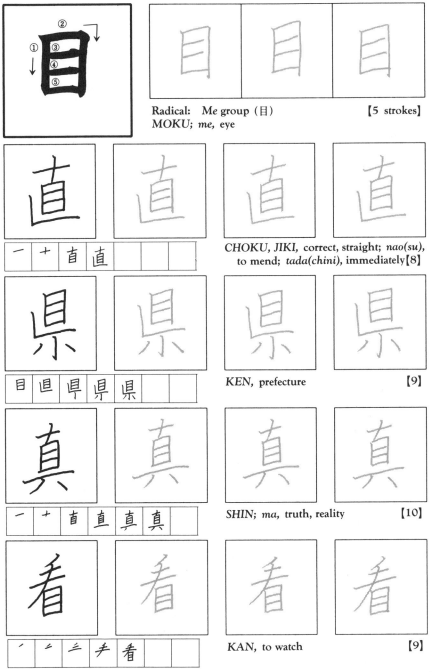

Radical: Me group (目)
MOKU; me, eye

【5 strokes】

一 十 直 直

CHOKU, JIKI, correct, straight; nao(su),
to mend; tada(chini), immediately【8】

目 旧 県 県 県

KEN, prefecture 【9】

一 十 直 直 真 真

SHIN; ma, truth, reality 【10】

丿 二 三 手 看

KAN, to watch 【9】

115

63. "And" group characters

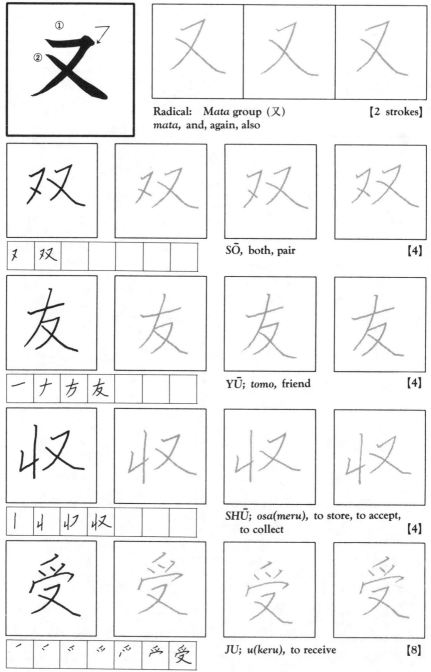

Radical: *Mata* group (又)   【2 strokes】
mata, and, again, also

SŌ, both, pair   【4】

YŪ; *tomo*, friend   【4】

SHŪ; *osa(meru)*, to store, to accept, to collect   【4】

JU; *u(keru)*, to receive   【8】

64. "Ship" group characters

Radical: *Fune-hen* (舟)   [6 strokes]
SHŪ; *fune*, boat, ship

SEN; *fune*, *-bune*, *funa-*, boat, ship 【11】

HAKU, *-PAKU*; *fune*, sea boat, ocean
liner 【11】

KŌ, to sail 【10】

HAN, to carry, to enjoy, to turn 【10】

65. "Two swords" group characters

Radical: *Rittō* group (刂)   [7 strokes]
BETSU, different; *waka(reru)*, to part from

ka(ru), to mow, to cut (hair)   [4]

KAN, publication, edition   [5]

RETSU, row, line   [6]

HAN, to divide into, to distinguish,
to decide; -BAN, size   [7]

66. "Standing heart" group characters

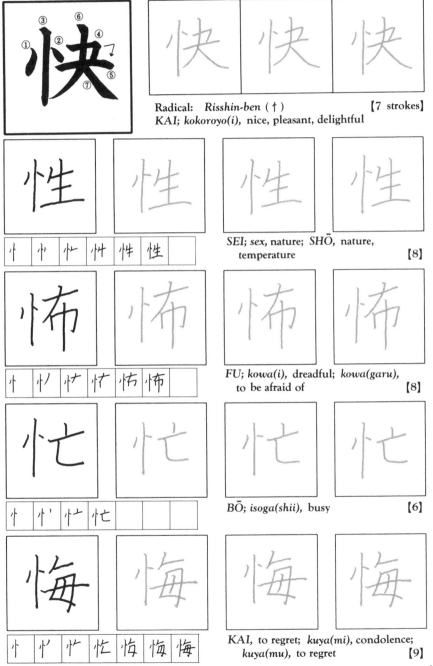

Radical: *Risshin-ben* (忄)   【7 strokes】
KAI; *kokoroyo(i)*, nice, pleasant, delightful

SEI; *sex*, nature; *SHŌ*, nature,
  temperature   【8】

FU; *kowa(i)*, dreadful; *kowa(garu)*,
  to be afraid of   【8】

BŌ; *isoga(shii)*, busy   【6】

KAI, to regret; *kuya(mi)*, condolence;
  kuya(mu), to regret   【9】

119

Exercise 11

Seiyō Bijutsu-kan   National Museum of Western Art

Keizai Kikaku-chō   Economic Planning Agency

kyūryō seikatsusha   salaried worker

nisetai jūtaku   a house for two families

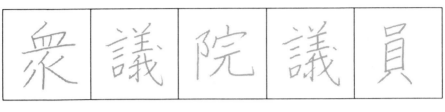

shūgi-in giin　member of the House of Representatives

uchū-hikōshi　astronaut

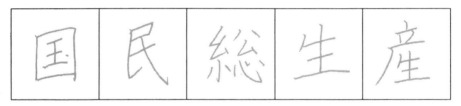

kokumin sō-seisan　gross national product

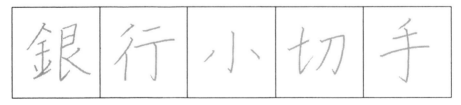

ginkō kogitte　bank check

67. "Roof and left wing" group characters

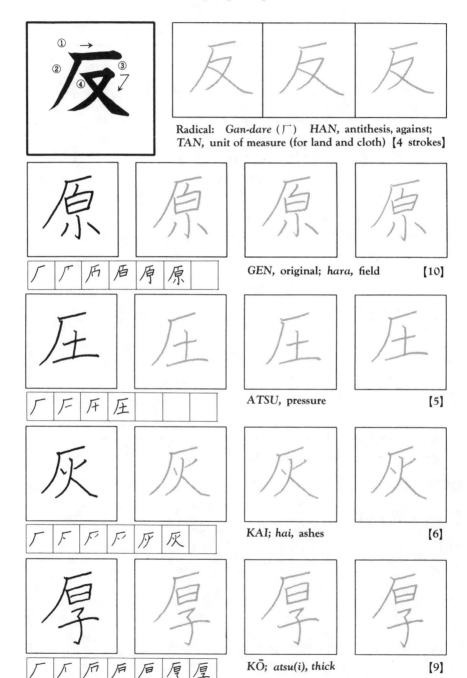

Radical: *Gan-dare* (厂) HAN, antithesis, against;
TAN, unit of measure (for land and cloth) [4 strokes]

厂 厂 厈 盾 原 原

GEN, original; *hara*, field [10]

厂 厂 圧 圧

ATSU, pressure [5]

厂 厂 厂 厂 灰 灰

KAI; *hai*, ashes [6]

厂 厂 厈 盾 厚 厚 厚

KŌ; *atsu(i)*, thick [9]

68. "Cow" group characters

Radical: *Ushi-hen* (牛)   **[4 strokes]**
GYŪ; *ushi*, cow, bull

BUTSU, MOTSU; *mono*, thing, article   **[8]**

BOKU; *maki*, stock farm, pasture   **[8]**

TOKU, special   **[10]**

SEI, sacrifice, victim   **[9]**

69. "Shell" group characters

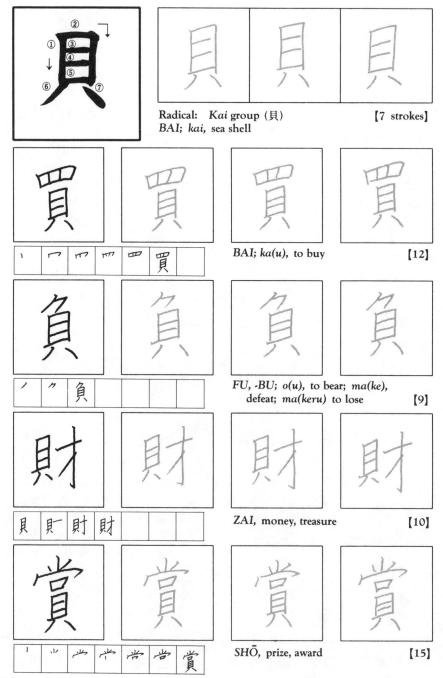

Radical: *Kai* group (貝)   【7 strokes】
BAI; *kai*, sea shell

BAI; *ka(u)*, to buy   【12】

FU, -BU; *o(u)*, to bear; *ma(ke)*, defeat; *ma(keru)* to lose   【9】

ZAI, money, treasure   【10】

SHŌ, prize, award   【15】

70. "Horse" group characters

Radical: *Uma-hen* (馬)

【10 strokes】

BA; *uma*, horse

馬 | 馬一 | 馬フ | 馬又 | 馬区

KU; *ka(ru)*, *ka(keru)*, to run, to gallop
【14】

馬 | 馬` | 馬＇ | 馬† | 駐≠ | 駐

CHŪ, to stop, to stay 【15】

馬 | 馬⁊ | 馬⁊ | 駅 | 駅

EKI, station 【14】

馬 | 駅 | 駼 | 駱 | 騒 | 騒 | 騒

SŌ; *sawa(gi)*, noise, disturbance;
sawa(gu), to make a noise 【18】

71. "Enclosed by three fences" group characters

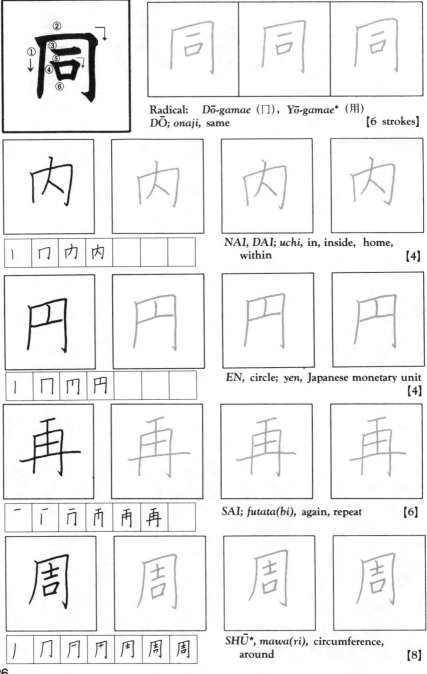

Radical: *Dō-gamae* (冂), *Yō-gamae** (用)
DŌ; *onaji*, same   [6 strokes]

NAI, DAI; *uchi*, in, inside, home,
     within   [4]

EN, circle; *yen*, Japanese monetary unit
                                               [4]

SAI; *futata(bi)*, again, repeat   [6]

SHŪ*, *mawa(ri)*, circumference,
     around   [8]

72. "Large" group characters

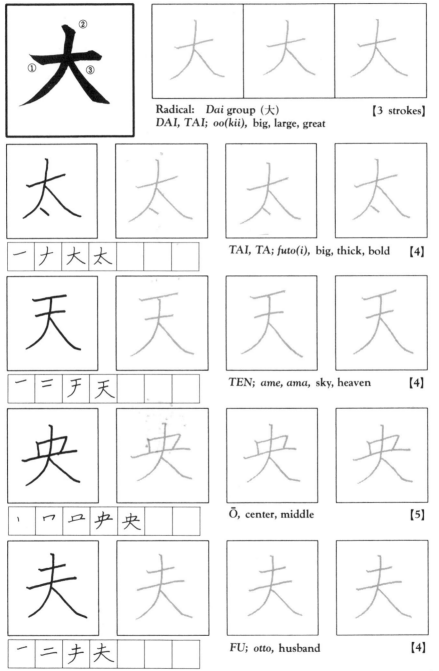

Radical: *Dai* group (大) **[3 strokes]**
DAI, TAI; *oo(kii)*, big, large, great

一 ナ 大 太

TAI, TA; *futo(i)*, big, thick, bold **[4]**

一 二 尹 天

TEN; *ame, ama*, sky, heaven **[4]**

丶 冂 冂 央 央

Ō, center, middle **[5]**

一 二 夫 夫

FU; *otto*, husband **[4]**

Exercise 12

(1) (2) (3) (4)

1. *bankoku hakurankai*   international exposition
2. *tentai-bōenkyō*   astronomical telescope
3. *genshiryoku hatsuden*   nuclear power generation
4. *josei shūkan-shi*   women's weekly magazine

(5) (6) (7) (8)

5. *kekkon kōshinkyoku* wedding march
6. *Shōkō Kaigisho* the Chamber of Commerce and Industry
7. *mibun-shōmeisho* identification card
8. *kokusai mihon-ichi* international trade fair

73. "Open box" group characters

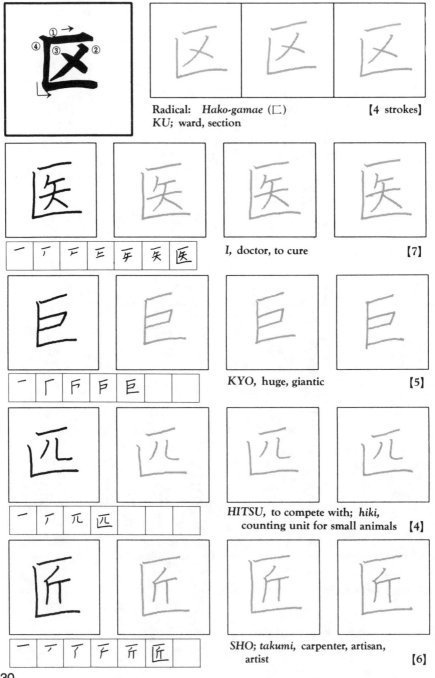

Radical: *Hako-gamae* (匚)   【4 strokes】
KU; ward, section

I, doctor, to cure   【7】

KYO, huge, giantic   【5】

HITSU, to compete with; *hiki*,
counting unit for small animals   【4】

SHO; *takumi*, carpenter, artisan,
artist   【6】

74. "Muscle power" group characters

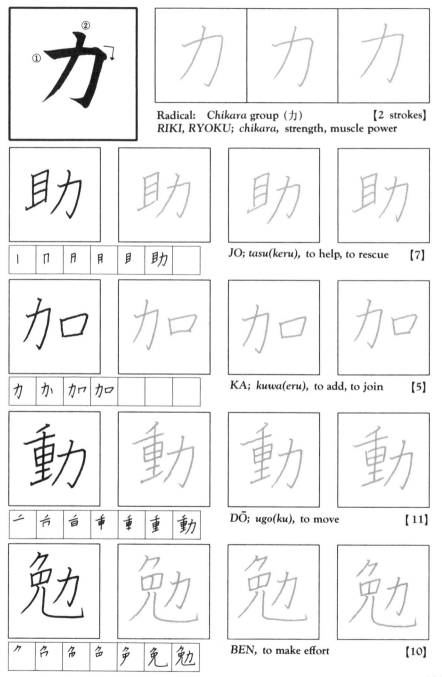

Radical: *Chikara* group (力) 【2 strokes】
RIKI, RYOKU; chikara, strength, muscle power

JO; *tasu(keru),* to help, to rescue 【7】

KA; *kuwa(eru),* to add, to join 【5】

DŌ; *ugo(ku),* to move 【11】

BEN, to make effort 【10】

75. "Running" group characters

Radical: Sō-nyo (走) 【7 strokes】
SŌ; hashi(ru), to run

KI; o(kiru), to rise, to get up 【10】

CHŌ, super- 【12】

ETSU; ko(eru), to go over, to exceed 【12】

SHU; omomuki, taste, effect, charm, air 【15】

76. "Eight" group characters

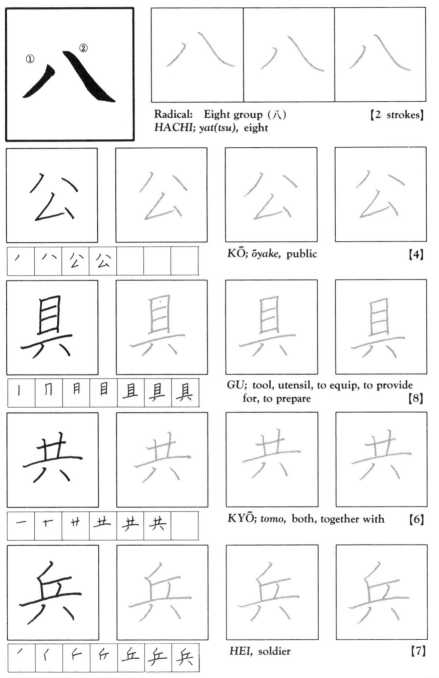

Radical: Eight group (八)   【2 strokes】
HACHI; *yat(tsu)*, eight

KŌ; ōyake, public   【4】

GU; tool, utensil, to equip, to provide
     for, to prepare   【8】

KYŌ; tomo, both, together with   【6】

HEI, soldier   【7】

77. "Flag" group characters

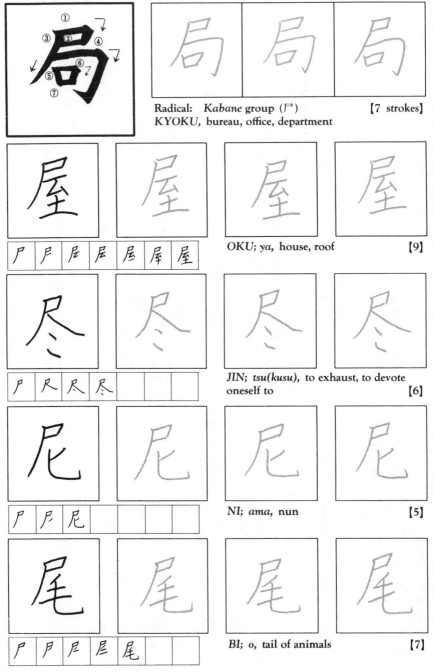

Radical: *Kabane* group (尸)　　　　[7 strokes]
KYOKU, bureau, office, department

OKU; *ya*, house, roof　　　　[9]

JIN; *tsu(kusu)*, to exhaust, to devote
oneself to　　　　[6]

NI; *ama*, nun　　　　[5]

BI; *o*, tail of animals　　　　[7]

78. "Death" group characters

Radical: *Ichita-hen* (歹)　　　　　[6 strokes]
SHI, death; *shi(nu)*, to die

ZAN; *noko(ri)*, remainder, balance;
　　noko(ru), to remain　　　　　[10]

SHU; *koto(ni)*, especially　　　　[10]

JUN, self-immolation (of an attendant
　　on the death of his lord)　　　[10]

SHOKU, to increase, to plant　　　[12]

135

Exercise 13

(1)   (2)   (3)   (4)

1. *jidōsha hoken*   automobile liability insurance
2. *ten'nen kinen-butsu*   natural monument
3. *daihyō torishimari-yaku*   president of a company
4. *teiki-jōshaken*   commuter pass

(5)   (6)   (7)   (8)

5. *Beikoku taishi-kan*   **American Embassy**
6. *kenchō shozaichi*   prefectural seat
7. *yūbin-kyoku madoguchi*   a window of a post office
8. *gakushū-sankōsho*   reference book for study

79. "Human" group characters

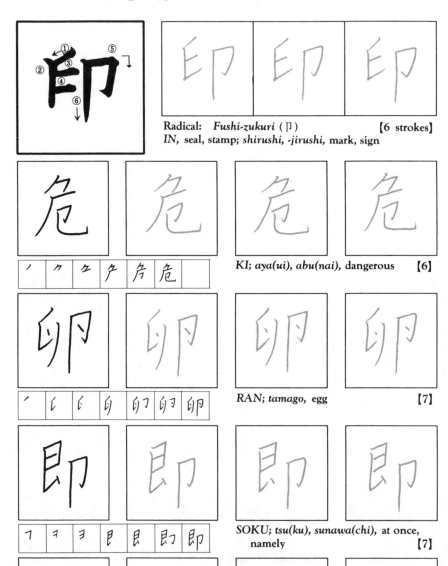

Radical: *Fushi-zukuri* (卩) [6 strokes]
IN, seal, stamp; *shirushi, -jirushi,* mark, sign

KI; *aya(ui), abu(nai),* dangerous [6]

RAN; *tamago,* egg [7]

SOKU; *tsu(ku), sunawa(chi),* at once,
namely [7]

KYAKU; to reject, to withdraw [7]

138

80. "Ice" group characters

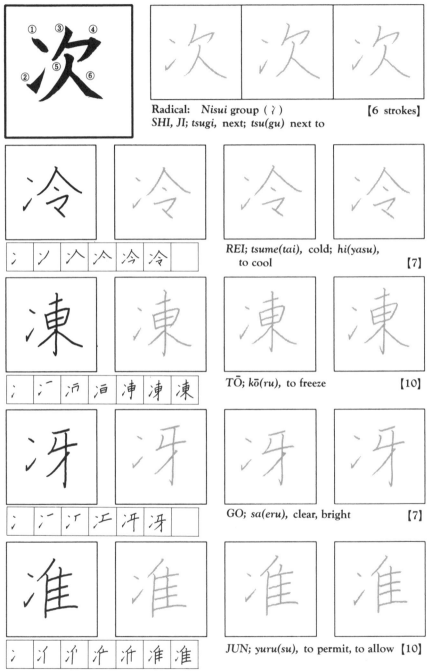

Radical: *Nisui* group (冫) [6 strokes]
SHI, JI; *tsugi*, next; *tsu(gu)* next to

REI; *tsume(tai)*, cold; *hi(yasu)*,
　　　to cool　　　　　　　　　　　　【7】

TŌ; *kō(ru)*, to freeze　　　　　　　【10】

GO; *sa(eru)*, clear, bright　　　　　【7】

JUN; *yuru(su)*, to permit, to allow 【10】

139

81. "Wide open mouth" group characters

Radical: *Akubi* group (欠) **[4 strokes]**
KETSU, lack, absence; *ka(keru),* to lack, to break off

KA; *uta,* song; *uta(u),* to sing **[14]**

Ō, Europe **[8]**

KIN, GON; *yoroko(bi),* joy, pleasure [8]

YOKU; *hos(suru),* to desire, to want
[11]

82. "Three diagonal strokes" group characters

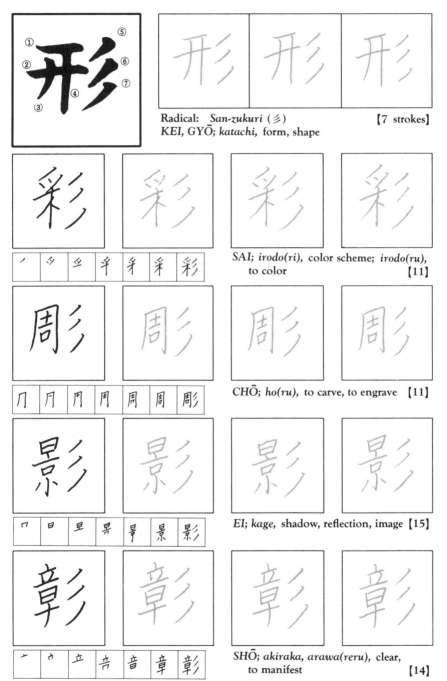

Radical: *San-zukuri* (彡) 【7 strokes】
KEI, GYŌ; *katachi,* form, shape

一 夕 尐 平 乎 采 彩

SAI; *irodo(ri),* color scheme; *irodo(ru),* to color 【11】

冂 月 冃 周 周 周 彫

CHŌ; *ho(ru),* to carve, to engrave 【11】

冂 日 旦 昮 昙 景 影

EI; *kage,* shadow, reflection, image 【15】

一 亠 立 咅 音 章 彰

SHŌ; *akiraka, arawa(reru),* clear, to manifest 【14】

83. "Weapon" group characters

Radical: *Rumata* group (殳)
SATSU, -SAI; *koro(su)*, to kill

【10 strokes】

Ō; *nagu(ru)*, to beat, to strike 【8】

DAN; step, grade 【9】

KAKU; *kara*, shell, valve, husk 【11】

KOKU, grain, cereal, corn 【14】

84. "Small shelf on the top" group characters

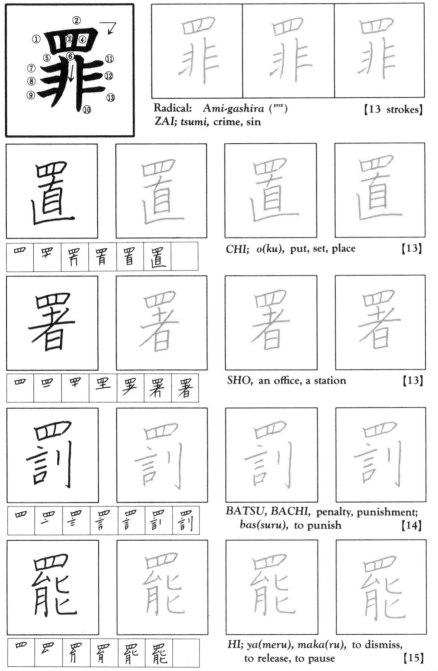

Radical: *Ami-gashira* (罒)   **[13 strokes]**
ZAI; *tsumi,* crime, sin

CHI; *o(ku),* put, set, place   **[13]**

SHO, an office, a station   **[13]**

BATSU, BACHI, penalty, punishment;
  bas(suru), to punish   **[14]**

HI; *ya(meru), maka(ru),* to dismiss,
  to release, to pause   **[15]**

143

85. "Day" (variation) group characters

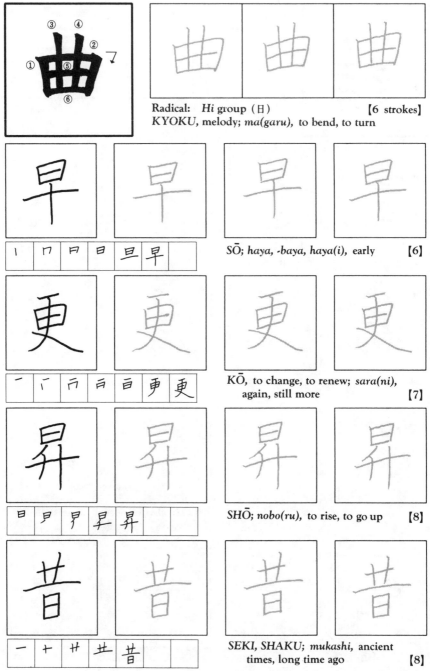

Radical: *Hi* group (日) [6 strokes]
KYOKU, melody; *ma(garu)*, to bend, to turn

SŌ; *haya, -baya, haya(i)*, early [6]

KŌ, to change, to renew; *sara(ni)*,
again, still more [7]

SHŌ; *nobo(ru)*, to rise, to go up [8]

SEKI, SHAKU; *mukashi*, ancient
times, long time ago [8]

86. "Stop" group characters

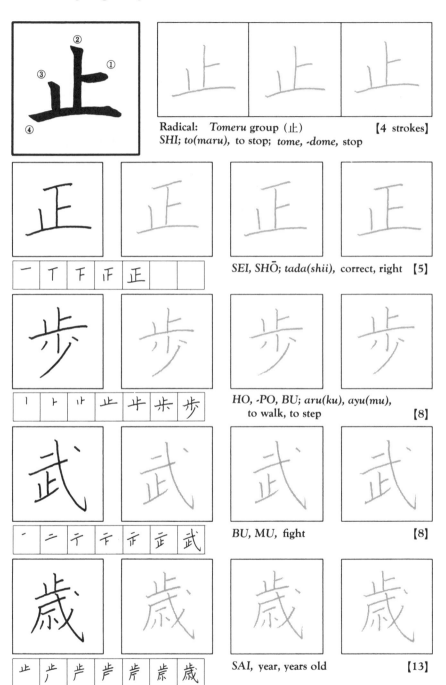

Radical: *Tomeru* group (止) [4 strokes]
SHI; *to(maru)*, to stop; *tome, -dome,* stop

一 丁 下 正 正

SEI, SHŌ; *tada(shii)*, correct, right [5]

丨 卜 卟 止 歩 歩 歩

HO, -PO, BU; *aru(ku), ayu(mu)*,
   to walk, to step [8]

一 二 千 千 千 武 武

BU, MU, fight [8]

止 广 芦 芦 芦 歳 歳

SAI, year, years old [13]

145

87. "Pike" group characters

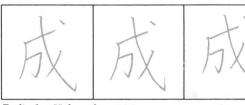

Radical: *Hoko-zukuri* (戈)　　　　　【6 strokes】
SEI, JŌ; *na(ru)*, to become, to be completed

一　二　干　开　戒　戒　戒

KAI; *imashi(meru)*, to admonish　　【7】

ノ　一　千　手　我　我　我

GA; *ware*, oneself, I　　　　　　　【7】

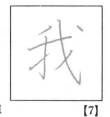

ソ　ハ　肖　当　単　戦　戦

SEN; *tataka(i)*, war, fight; *tataka(u)*,
　to fight　　　　　　　　　　　　【13】

ｌ　ｆ　ｒ　ゲ　虍　虚　戯

GI, fun, play; *tawamu(reru)*, to play,
　to joke, to sport　　　　　　　　【15】

88. More complicated characters (1)

Radical: *Ki-hen* [16 strokes]
KI; *hata*; loom, mechanism

Radical: *Tobu* group [9]
HI; *to(bu)*, to fly

Radical: *Gyō-gamae* [16]
EI, to protect, to defend

Radical: *Sanzui* [15]
KETSU; *isagiyo(i)*, brave, pure, clean

Radical: *Ito-hen* [18]
SHOKU, SHIKI; *o(ru)*, to weave

147

89. More complicated characters (2)

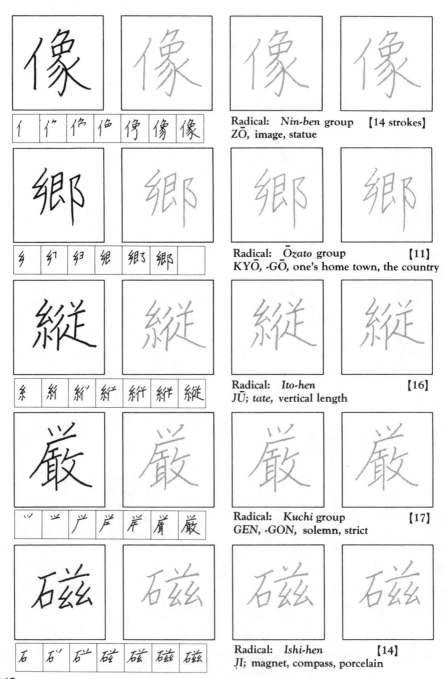

Radical: *Nin-ben* group 【14 strokes】
ZŌ, image, statue

Radical: *Ōzato* group 【11】
KYŌ, -GŌ, one's home town, the country

Radical: *Ito-hen* 【16】
JŪ; *tate*, vertical length

Radical: *Kuchi* group 【17】
GEN, -GON, solemn, strict

Radical: *Ishi-hen* 【14】
JI; magnet, compass, porcelain

90. More complicated characters (3)

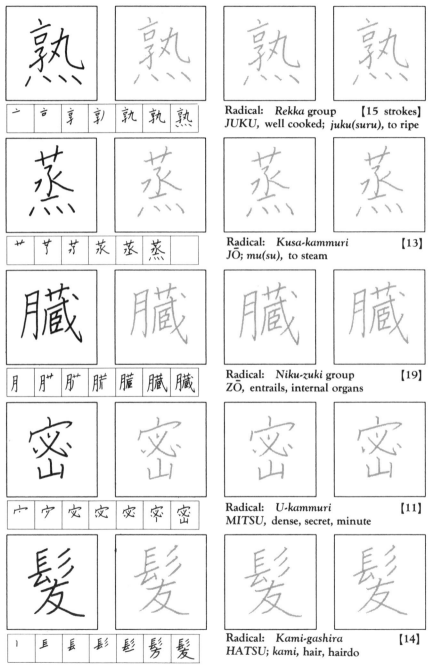

Radical: *Rekka* group   [15 strokes]
JUKU, well cooked; *juku(suru)*, to ripe

Radical: *Kusa-kammuri*   【13】
JŌ; *mu(su)*, to steam

Radical: *Niku-zuki* group   【19】
ZŌ, entrails, internal organs

Radical: *U-kammuri*   【11】
MITSU, dense, secret, minute

Radical: *Kami-gashira*   【14】
HATSU; *kami*, hair, hairdo

Exercise Sheet   Date: Name:

● Copy this page to use as an exercise sheet.

Chapter 2

You have studied the writing of basic *kanji* characters in the first chapter. In the second chapter, you will study practical sentences written with *kanji* together with *hiragana* and *katakana*, such as those Japanese write in their daily life.

In this chapter, all of the characters in squares are written with dotted lines. Trace over the lines and complete the sentences. You must practice writing these words and sentences repeatedly on your own paper or on copies of the exercise sheets at the end of this book* Each short sentence includes at least one common Japanese family name. You can learn more than 20 common Japanese family names by practicing these sentences. Additionally, common Japanese proverbs teach you several lessons based on the wisdom and experience of the people of old Japan.

Charts of *hiragana* and *katakana* are at the beginning of this chapter. The stroke order for each *kana* is omitted, as you should have already learned *hiragana* and *katakana* before learning *kanji.*

The proper way to address an envelope or postcard is probably useful for you when sending a letter to a Japanese friend. Your Japanese will improve greatly if you use Japanese as much as possible when writing to your Japanese friends. The more you use Japanese, the more your language skills will improve.

* (There is an additional exercise sheet at the end of Chapter 1.)

BASIC HIRAGANA

あ	か	さ	た	な
a	*ka*	*sa*	*ta*	*na*
い	き	し	ち	に
i	*ki*	*shi*	*chi*	*ni*
う	く	す	つ	ぬ
u	*ku*	*su*	*tsu*	*nu*
え	け	せ	て	ね
e	*ke*	*se*	*te*	*ne*
お	こ	そ	と	の
o	*ko*	*so*	*to*	*no*

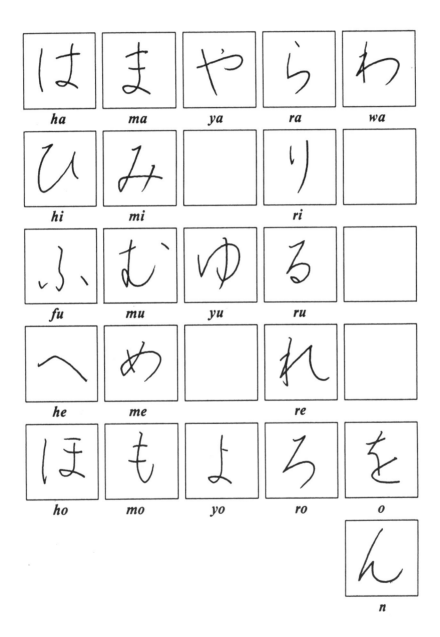

は	ま	や	ら	わ
ha	*ma*	*ya*	*ra*	*wa*
ひ	み		り	
hi	*mi*		*ri*	
ふ	む	ゆ	る	
fu	*mu*	*yu*	*ru*	
へ	め		れ	
he	*me*		*re*	
ほ	も	よ	ろ	を
ho	*mo*	*yo*	*ro*	*o*
				ん
				n

BASIC KATAKANA

ア	カ	サ	タ	ナ
a	*ka*	*sa*	*ta*	*na*
イ	キ	シ	チ	ニ
i	*ki*	*shi*	*chi*	*ni*
ウ	ク	ス	ツ	ヌ
u	*ku*	*su*	*tsu*	*nu*
エ	ケ	セ	テ	ネ
e	*ke*	*se*	*te*	*ne*
オ	コ	ソ	ト	ノ
o	*ko*	*so*	*to*	*no*

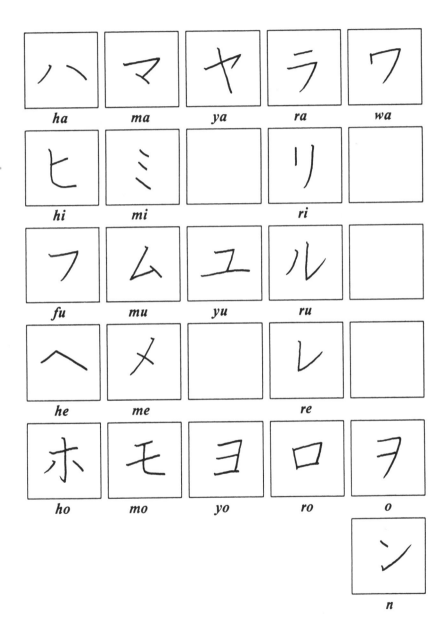

ハ *ha*	マ *ma*	ヤ *ya*	ラ *ra*	ワ *wa*
ヒ *hi*	ミ *mi*		リ *ri*	
フ *fu*	ム *mu*	ユ *yu*	ル *ru*	
ヘ *he*	メ *me*		レ *re*	
ホ *ho*	モ *mo*	ヨ *yo*	ロ *ro*	ヲ *o*
				ン *n*

155

Short Sentences with Kanji

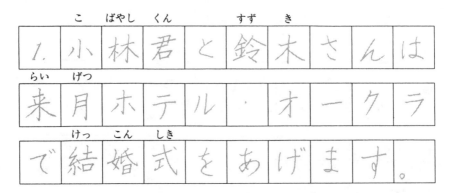

Kobayashi-kun to Suzuki-san wa rai-getsu Hoteru Ōkura de kekkon-shiki o agemasu.

Mr. Kobayashi and Ms. Suzuki will hold their wedding ceremony next month at the Hotel Okura.

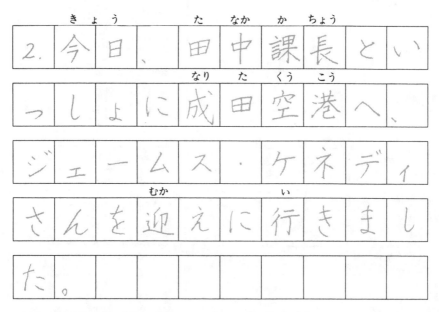

Kyō, Tanaka-kachō to issho ni Narita Kūkō e, Jēmusu Kenedi-san o mukae ni ikimashita.

Today, I went with Manager Tanaka to Narita Airport to greet Mr. James Kennedy.

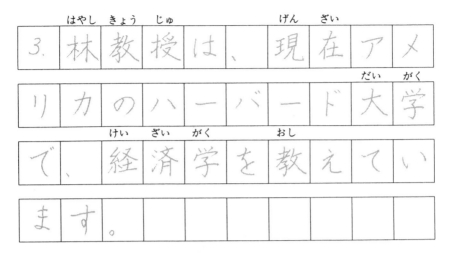

3. 林教授は、現在アメリカのハーバード大学で、経済学を教えています。

Hayashi-kyōju wa, genzai Amerika no Hābādo Daigaku de, keizai-gaku o oshiete imasu.

Presently, Professor Hayashi is teaching economics at Harvard University.

4. 「クラークさん、野球はお好きですか」
「ええ、好きです。今度の日曜日に、横浜ライオンズというチームとゲームをやります。

157

ぜひ応援に来てくださ

い」

"Kurāku-san, yakyū wa osuki desu ka?"
"Ee, suki desu. Kondo no nichiyō-bi ni, Yokohama Raionzu to iu chīmu to gēmu o yarimasu. Zehi ōen ni kite kudasai."

"Do you like baseball, Mr. Clark?"
"Yes, I do. Next Sunday we have a game with a team called the Yokohama Lions. By all means, please come and support the team."

5. 私は松本清張の推理
小説のファンです。イ
ギリスの作家ではディ
ック・フランシスの作
品をよく読みます。

Watashi wa Matsumoto Seichō no suiri-shōsetsu no fan desu. Igirisu no sakka de wa Dikku Furanshisu no sakuhin o yoku yomimasu.

I am a fan of Seichō Matsumoto's detective stories. As for English writers, I often read Dick Francis' books.

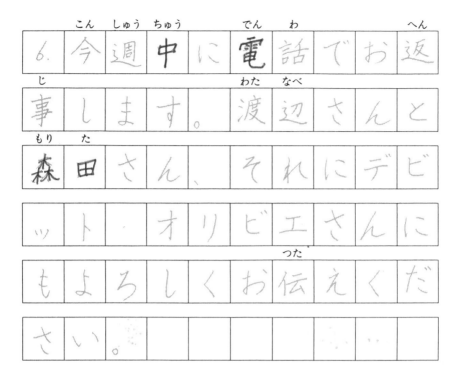

6. 今週中に電話でお返事します。渡辺さんと森田さん、それにデビット・オリビエさんにもよろしくお伝えください。

Konshū-chū ni denwa de ohenji shimasu. Watanabe-san to Morita-san, sore ni Debitto Oribie-san ni mo yoroshiku otsutae kudasai.

I'll reply by telephone sometime this week. Please give my regards to Mr. Watanabe, Ms. Morita and David Olivier.

7. 伊藤さんはかぜで、石川さんは仕事の都合で、ディズニーランド

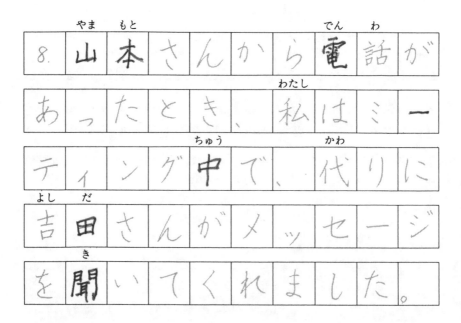

ドに遊びにいけませんでした。

Itō-san wa kaze de, Ishikawa-san wa shigoto no tsugō de, Dizunī Rando ni asobi ni ikemasen deshita.

Because Mr. Itō had a cold and Ms. Ishikawa was busy with her work, they could not go to Disneyland.

8. 山本さんから電話があったとき、私はミーティング中で、代りに吉田さんがメッセージを聞いてくれました。

Yamamoto-san kara denwa ga atta toki, watashi wa mītingu-chū de, kawari ni Yoshida-san ga messēji o kiite kuremashita.

I was in a meeting when Ms. Yamamoto called, so Mr. Yoshida took a message for me.

9. 日本の総理大臣は小川氏で、外務大臣は佐藤氏です。現在イタリアで開催中のサミットに出席しています。

Nippon no Sōri-Daijin wa Ogawa-shi de, Gaimu-Daijin wa Satō-shi desu. Genzai Itaria de kaisai-chū no samitto ni shusseki shiteimasu.

Japan's Prime Minister is Mr. Ogawa, and the Foreign Minister is Mr. Satō. Presently, they are attending a summit in Italy.

10. 斎藤さんは三月に大学を卒業して、ドイツのフランクフルト大学に留学しました。

Saitō-san wa san-gatsu ni daigaku o sotsugyō shite, Doitsu no Furankufuruto Daigaku ni ryūgaku shimashita.

Ms. Saitō graduated from the university in March, then studied overseas in Germany at the University of Frankfurt.

	私	の	趣	味	は	ロ	ッ	ク	・
_11._	わたし		しゅ	み					

Reading: 11. 私の趣味はロック・クライミングですが、親友の高橋君はスキューバ・ダイビングに熱中しています。

Watashi no shumi wa rokku kuraimingu desu ga, shin'yū no Taka-hashi-kun wa sukyūba daibingu ni netchū shite imasu.

One of my hobbies is rock climbing, but my close friend Mr. Taka-hashi is very interested in scuba diving.

12. 「石川さんの家はレストランで、加藤君の家は肉屋です。ジェフ

のお父さんは何をして
いますか」
「私の父はサラリーマ
ンです」

"Ishikawa-san no ie wa resutoran de, Katō-kun no ie wa niku-ya desu. Jefu no otōsan wa nani o shite imasu ka?"
"Watashi no chichi wa sararīman desu."

"Ms. Ishikawa's family runs a restaurant, and Mr. Kato's owns a butcher shop. What does your father do, Jeff?"
"My father is a white-collar worker."

13.「東海道新幹線で京
都見物に行って来まし
た」「加藤さん、ひと
りで行ったのですか」
「いいえ五人で行きま

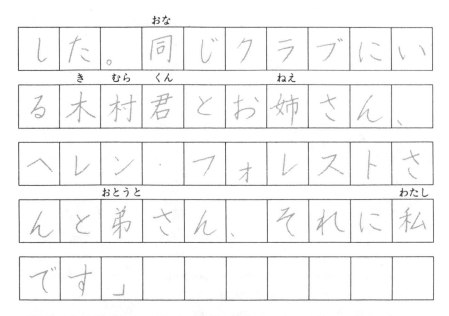

した。同じクラブにい
る木村君とお姉さん、
ヘレン・フォレストさ
んと弟さん、それに私
です」

"Tōkaidō Shinkansen de Kyōto kenbutsu ni itte kimashita."
"Katō-san, hitori de itta no desu ka?"
"Iie go-nin de ikimashita.Onaji kurabu ni iru Kimura-kun to onēsan,
Heren Horesuto-san to otōtosan, sore ni watashi desu."

"I took the Tokaido Bullet Train to see the sights in Kyoto."
"Did you go by yourself, Ms. Kato?"
"No, five of us went. Mr. Kimura and his older sister, who are in the
same club as I am, Helen Forrest and her younger brother, and me."

14.「クラスで、いちば
ん背の高いのは山田君
で、低いのは中島さん
です」「いちばんの美

|人|は|だ|れ|で|す|か|」|「|中|
|村|さ|ん|で|す|」||||||

furigana: 人 = じん, 中 = なか, 村 = むら

"Kurasu de, ichiban sei no takai no wa Yamada-kun de, hikui no wa Nakajima-san desu."
"Ichiban no bijin wa dare desu ka?"
"Nakamura-san desu."

"The tallest in the class is Mr. Yamada, and the shortest is Ms. Nakajima."
"Who is the most attractive?"
"Ms. Nakamura."

15.	就	職	し	て	か	ら	は	友	だ
ち	が	み	ん	な	遠	く	に	住	ん
で	い	る	の	で	、	な	か	な	か
会	え	な	い	。	山	口	は	ニ	ュ
ー	ヨ	ー	ク	、	長	谷	川	は	パ
リ	、	井	上	さ	ん	は	ベ	ル	リ

furigana: 就職 = しゅう しょく, 遠 = とお, 住 = す, 会 = あ, 山口 = やま ぐち, 長谷川 = は せ がわ, 井上 = いの うえ

165

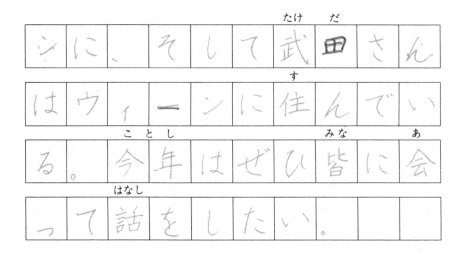

Shūshoku shite kara wa tomodachi ga minna tōku ni sunde iru node, nakanaka aenai. Yamaguchi wa Nyūyōku, Hasegawa wa Pari, Inoue-san wa Berurin ni, soshite Takeda-san wa Uīn ni sunde iru. Kotoshi wa zehi mina ni atte hanashi o shitai.

Since we started working, my friends all live far away and we rarely have a chance to meet. Yamaguchi is in New York, Hasegawa in Paris, Ms. Inoue is in Berlin and Ms. Takeda lives in Vienna. I really want to meet and talk with them this year.

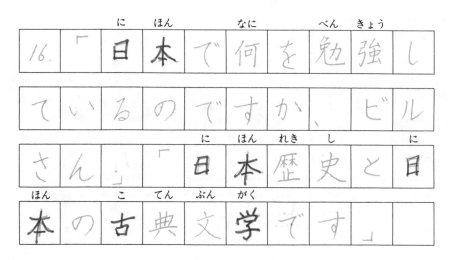

「暇な時はテレビを見たり、ラジオを聞いたりしますか」「私はどちらかというと、じっとしているより体を動かすほうが好きです。時間があれば、柔道の練習に行きます」

"Nihon de nani o benkyō shiteiru no desu ka, Biru-san?"
"Nihon rekishi to Nihon no koten bungaku desu."
"Hima na toki wa terebi o mitari, rajio o kiitari shimasu ka?"
"Watashi wa dochira ka to iu to, jitto shite iru yori karada o ugokasu hō ga suki desu. Jikan ga areba Jūdō no renshū ni ikimasu."

"What are you studying in Japan, Bill?"
"Japanese history and classical literature."
"Do you watch television and listen to the radio in your free time?"
"I prefer active hobbies to more leisurely ones. If I have time, I practice judo."

Japanese Proverbs

四、地獄の沙汰も金次第

地獄の沙汰も金次第

Jigoku no sata mo kane shidai.

三、大は小を兼ねる

大は小を兼ねる

Dai wa shō o kaneru.

二、犬も歩けば棒にあたる

犬も歩けば棒にあたる

Inu mo arukeba bō ni ataru.

一、案ずるより生むが易い

案ずるより生むが易い

Anzuru yori umu ga yasui.

168

八、二階から目薬

二階から目薬

Ni-kai kara me-gusuri.

七、七転び八起き

七転び八起き

Nana korobi ya oki.

六、灯台下暗し

灯台下暗し

Tōdai moto kurashi.

五、出る杭は打たれる

出る杭は打たれる

Deru kui wa utareru.

十二、安物買いの銭失い　*Yasumono-gai no zeni ushinai.*

安物買いの銭失い

十一、目は口ほどに物を言う　*Me wa kuchi hodo ni mono o iu.*

目は口ほどに物を言う

十、残り物には福がある　*Nokori-mono ni wa fuku ga aru.*

残り物には福がある

九、逃がした魚は大きい　*Nigashita sakana wa ōkii.*

逃がした魚は大きい

六、猿も木から落ちる

Saru mo ki kara ochiru.

猿も木から落ちる

二七、朱に交われば赤くなる

Shu ni majiwareba akaku naru.

朱に交われば赤くなる

二八、百聞は一見に如かず

Hyaku-bun wa i-kken ni shikazu.

百聞は一見に如かず

二九、論より証拠

Ron yori shōko.

論より証拠

171

二十、噂をすれば影がさす

Uwasa o sureba kage ga sasu.

十九、言わぬが花

Iwanu ga hana.

十八、会うは別れの初め

Au wa wakare no hajime.

十七、魚心あれば水心

Uo-gokoro areba mizu-gokoro.

二四、苦しい時の神だのみ

苦しい時の神だのみ

Kurushii toki no kami-danomi.

二三、腐っても鯛

腐っても鯛

Kusatte mo Tai.

二二、飼犬に手を嚙まれる

飼犬に手を嚙まれる

Kai-inu ni te o kamareru.

二一、鬼の留守に洗濯

鬼の留守に洗濯

Oni no rusu ni sentaku.

二十八、仏の顔も三度

Hotoke no kao mo san-do.

仏の顔も三度

二十七、人を呪えば穴二つ

Hito o noroeba ana futatsu.

人を呪えば穴二つ

二十六、花より団子

Hana yori dango.

花より団子

二十五、猫に小判

Neko ni koban.

猫に小判

三十二、去る者は日々*にうとし

Saru mono wa hibi ni utoshi.

去る者は日々にうとし

三十一、石の上にも三年

Ishi no ue ni mo san-nen.

石の上にも三年

三十、嘘も方便

Uso mo hōben.

嘘も方便

二十九、身から出た錆

Mi kara deta sabi.

身から出た錆

* 々 This symbol is used to repeat the sound of the character
preceding it.

1. Lit. Giving birth to a child is not as painful as worrying about it beforehand.

   Things may look more difficult than they really are.

2. a) Lit. A dog wandering about will be hit by a stick.

   Curiousity killed the cat.

   b) Lit. A dog wandering about will find a stick.

   A flying crow always catches something.

3. The greater serves the lesser.   The greater includes the lesser.

4. Lit. The sentence of death from hell is influenced by money.

   Money is the key that opens all doors.
   Money makes the mare go.

5. Lit. A tall stake is struck to the same level of other stakes.

   The nail that sticks out gets hammered down.

6. Lit. The lighthouse does not shine on its base.

   It is dark at the base of a candle.

7. Lit. Fall seven times, get up eight.

   The ups and downs of life.

8. Lit. That's like dropping eye lotion into someone's eyes from the second floor.

   That's like trying to find a needle in a haystack.

   That's like trying to pass a camel through the eye of a needle.

9. It is the fish you lose that are the biggest.

   Every fish that escapes appears to be bigger than it is.

10. Good things come to those who wait.

11. Eyes are as eloquent as the tongue.

    A glance can speak volumes.

12. Lit. Buy cheap and waste money.

    Penny wise and pound foolish.

13. Lit. Proof wins over argument.

    The proof of the pudding is in the eating.

14. Lit. One sight is better than one hundred sounds.
    Seeing is believing.   A picture is worth a thousand words.

15. Lit. The hand of a man who handles vermilion will become red.
    He that touches pitch shall be defiled.

16. Lit. Even monkeys fall from trees.
    Homer sometimes nods.   Best marksmen may miss.

17. Lit. If you wish to become a fish, I'll become water.
    Scratch my back and I'll scratch yours.

18. Lit. Meeting is the beginning of parting.
    We meet only to part.

19. Lit. Silence is a flower.
    Silence is golden.   Better left unsaid.

20. Lit. Speak of someone and he appears.
    Speak of the devil and he appears.

21. Lit. Relax in the absence of our fiendish supervisor.
    When the cats away, the mice will play.

22. Lit. To have one's hand bitten by one's own dog.
    Warm is the snake in one's bosom.   Bite the hand that feeds you.

23. Lit. A rotten sea bream is still worth more than other fish.
    An old eagle is better than a young crow.

24. Lit. One asks for God's help in times of trouble, then forgets God.
    Danger past, God forgotten.

25. Lit. To give a gold coin to a cat.   To cast pearls before swine.

26. Lit. Dumplings are better than blossoms.
    Pudding before praise.   Bread is better than songs of birds.

27. Lit. He who digs a pit for others falls in himself.
    Curses, like chickens, come home to roost.

28. Lit. The Buddha refuses those who ask three times unabashedly.
    There are limits to one's endurance.

29. Lit. The rust brought from within oneself.

   An ill life, an ill end.

30. Lit. A lie is sometimes useful.   White lies can be forgiven.

31. Lit. Endurance, such as sitting for three years on a rock, will
   bring success.

   Perseverance will win in the end.

32. Lit. We will forget the people left along the way.

   Out of sight, out of mind.

Reference work: *yuki* (snow) in Dynamic Calligraphy by Rika Sagano

Addressing a Letter in Japanese

When addressing an envelope or postcard, the writing system for one's name and address in Japanese is the reverse of that of English. The address is written before the name of the addressee, in order of scale from the largest geographic classification to the smallest. The largest areas to be written are: *to* (*Tōkyō-to,* 東京都, *Tokyo* Metropolitan Area); *fu* (*Ōsaka-fu* 大阪府, *Osaka* Prefecture; *Kyoto-fu* 京都府, *Kyoto* Prefecture); *dō* (*Hokkai-dō* 北海道, *Hokkaido* Prefecture), *ken* (ex. *Hiroshima-ken* 広島県, *Hiroshima* Prefecture).

Following them, the name of the city, (*shi* ex. *Okayama-shi* 岡山市), ward (*ku* 区), county (*gun* 郡), town (*chō, machi* 町), village (*son, mura* 村), village section (*aza* 字), block number (*chōme* 丁目) and house number are written in order from large to small. Not all addresses use all these terms. For large cities and in cases where the name of the city is same as the largest area name (ex. *Kyōto-fu, Kyōto-shi,* or *Akita-ken, Akita-shi*), the largest area name may be omitted. The zip code on the envelope is necessary to ensure prompt delivery.

Japanese names are written with the family name first, followed by the recipients's given name.

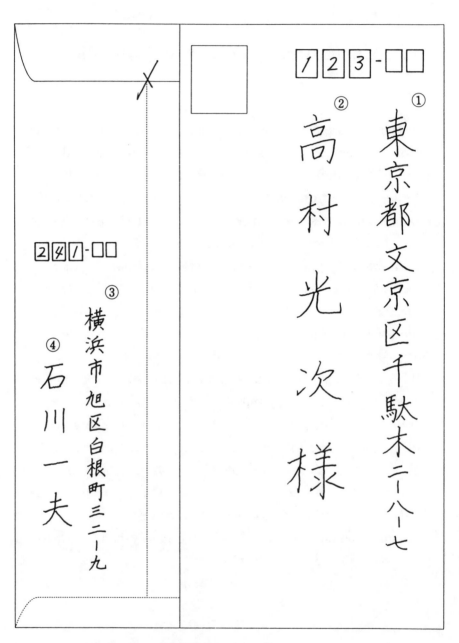

① 東京都文京区千駄木二－八－七

② 高村光次 様

③ 横浜市旭区白根町三二－九

④ 石川一夫

① *Tōkyō-to Bunkyō-ku Sendagi 2-8-7*

② *Takamura Kōji sama*

③ *Yokohama-shi Asahi-ku Shirane-chō 32-9*

④ *Ishikawa Kazuo*

123-□□

東京都文京区千駄木二一八一七

高村光次様

241-□□

横浜市旭区白根町三二一九

石川一夫

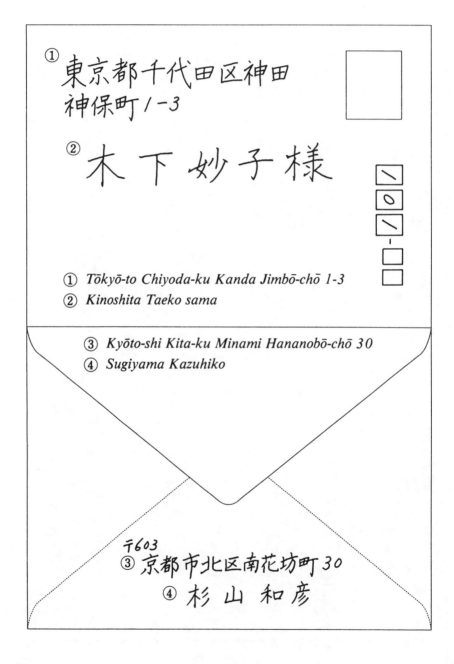

① 東京都千代田区神田
神保町 1-3

② 木下 妙子 様

① *Tōkyō-to Chiyoda-ku Kanda Jimbō-chō 1-3*
② *Kinoshita Taeko sama*

③ *Kyōto-shi Kita-ku Minami Hananobō-chō 30*
④ *Sugiyama Kazuhiko*

〒603
③ 京都市北区南花坊町 30
④ 杉 山 和彦

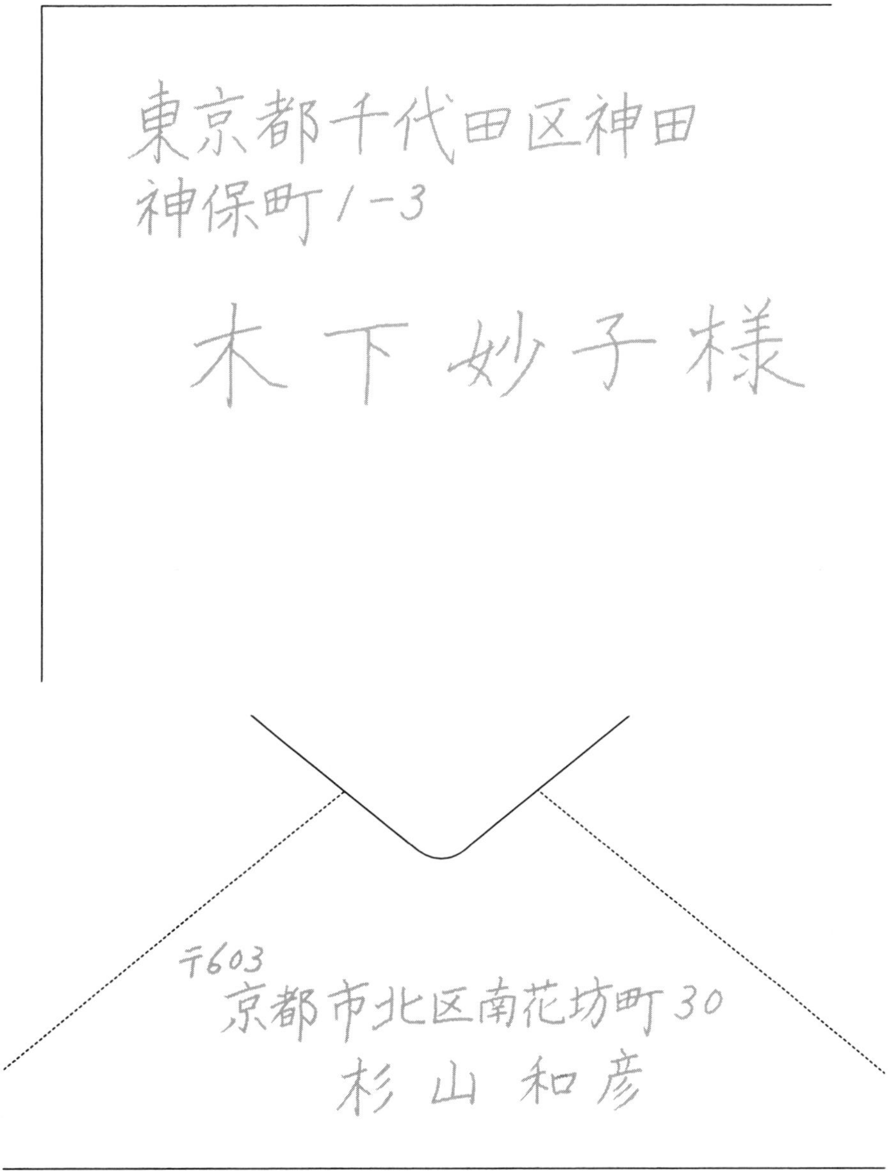

東京都千代田区神田
神保町1-3

　木下　妙子様

〒603
　京都市北区南花坊町30
　　杉山　和彦

New Year's Greeting Cards

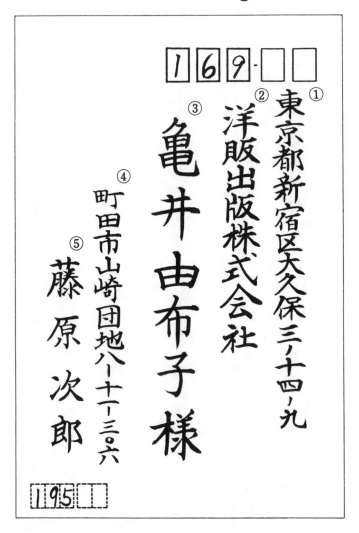

① Address: *Tōkyō-to Shinjuku-ku Ōkubo 3-14-9*
② Company's name: *Yōhan Shuppan Kabushiki Gaisha*
③ Recipient's name: *Kamei Yukō sama* (Miss)
④ Sender's address: *Machida-shi Yamazaki Danchi 8-11-306*
⑤ Sender's name: *Fujiwara Jirō*

185

①謹賀新年

②一月一日

③東京都世田谷区祖師谷三ノ八
キングマンション一〇五

④大森 利彦

① I wish you a Happy New Year.
② January 1st
③ Sender's address: *Tōkyō-to Setagaya-ku Soshigaya 3-8*
   King Mansion #105
④ Sender's name: *Ōmori Toshihiko*

謹賀新年

一月一日

東京都世田谷区祖師谷三八

キングマンション一〇五

大森 利彦

① 謹んで新年の
ごあいさつを申しあげます

② 一九九四年 元旦

① I wish you a Happy New Year.
② New Year's Day, 1994

謹んで新年の
ごあいさつを申しあげます

一九九四年 元旦

① 明けまして
おめでとうございます

② 元旦

③ 田中　美佐子

④ 横須賀市深田八五

① I wish you a Happy New Year.
② New Year's Day
③ Sender's name:　*Tanaka Misako*
④ Sender's Address:　*Yokosuka-shi Fukada 85*

明けまして
おめでとうございます

元旦

田中 美佐子

横須賀市深田八五

191

Sample Letter (to a Friend)

玲子さん

東京はまだまだきびしい残暑が続いているでしょうね。今年の夏は三十年ぶりという特別な暑さでしたから。でもお家の皆さんは、お変りなく、お元気で毎日をお過しのことと思います。

先週、サンフランシスコに無事帰って参りましたので、ご安心ください。日本滞在中はいろいろとありがとうございました。楽しかった日本での生活は、私にとっていつまでも忘れられない、すばらしい思い出になるでしょう。

今度の冬休みには、ぜひこちらに遊びに来てください。クリスマスの休暇を、私の家族といっしょに過していただけたら、とても嬉しいです。

　それでは、ご両親や美恵と竜郎にもよろしくお伝えください。

　皆さんに、またお会いできる日を楽しみにしています。

1994年8月25日

リサ

Reiko-san

Tōkyō wa madamada kibishii zansho ga tsuzuite iru deshō ne. Ko-toshi no natsu wa san-ju-nen buri to iu, tokubetsu na atsusa deshita kara. Demo o-uchi no mina-san wa, o-kawari naku, o-genki de mai-nichi o o-sugoshi no koto to omoimasu.

Senshū, Sanfuranshisuko ni buji kaette mairimashita node, go-anshin kudasai. Nihon taizai-chū wa iroiro to arigatō-gozaimashita. Tanoshikatta Nihon deno seikatsu wa, watashi ni totte itsu made mo wasurerare nai, subarashii omoide ni naru deshō.

Kondo no fuyu-yasumi ni wa, zehi kochira ni asobi ni kite kudasai. Kurisumasu no kyūka o, watashi no kazoku to issho ni sugoshite itadaketara, totemo ureshii desu.

Soredewa, go-ryōshin ya Mie to Tatsuo ni mo yoroshiku o-tsutae kudasai. Minasan ni, mata o-ai dekiru hi o tanoshimi ni shiteimasu.

1994 nen 8 gatsu 25 nichi

Lisa

Dear Reiko,

I see the extreme heat still continues in Tokyo. This summer is said to be especially hot, the hottest in thirty years. But I expect your family is passing the days as healthy as ever.

Last week I returned safely to San Francisco, so please don't worry about me. Thank you for all you did for me during my time in Japan. I will never forget the happy times during my life in Japan—wonderful memories!

If it's at all possible, please come and visit during your winter vacation this year. I would be very happy if you would spend the Christmas holidays with my family.

Well, please say hello for me to your parents and Mie and Tatsuo. I am looking forward to the day we can all meet again.

August 25, 1994

Lisa

玲子さん

　東京はまだまだきび
しい残暑が続いている
でしょうね。今年の夏
は三十年ぶりという特
別な暑さでしたから。
でもお家の皆さんは、
お変りなく、お元気で
毎日をお過しのことと
思います。

　先週、サンフランシ
スコに無事帰って参り

ましたので、ご安心く
ださい。日本滞在中は
いろいろとありがとう
ございました。楽しか
った日本での生活は、
私にとっていつまでも
忘れられない、すばら
しい思い出になるでし
ょう。
　今度の冬休みには、
ぜひこちらに遊びに来
てください。クリスマ

スの休暇を、私の家族といっしょに過していただけたら、とても嬉しいです。

　それでは、ご両親や美恵と竜郎にもよろしくお伝えください。

　皆さんに、またお会いできる日を楽しみにしています。

1994年 8月 25日

リサ

On Radicals and Their Meanings

All *kanji* characters can be divided into groups based on their radicals. Each radical has its own meaning, and this meaning links all characters in same group. For example, the character 休 *(KYŪ, yasu(mu))* consists of two parts: the *nin-ben* radical (イ), meaning "people", and the character for tree (木). *Yasu(mu)* means "to rest", and if you use your imagination, you can see a person sitting under a tree.

To find a character's reading or meaning in a *Kanwa Jiten* (a Japanese *Kanji* dictionary), you would first locate that character's radical group. Characters within a given radical group are arranged by their number of strokes.

Reference work: *uma* (horse) in Dynamic Calligraphy by Rika Sagano

	Hen (–ben): Left-side radicals						
	name of radical	meaning					
イ(人)	nin-ben	people	休	体	作	何	仏
冫	nisui	freezing	次	冷	准	凍	凝
口	kuchi-hen	mouth	右	名	味	鳴	古
土	tsuchi-hen	ground	城	坂	地	場	埋
女	onna-hen	woman	姉	妹	始	好	妃
弓	yumi-hen	bow	引	強	弱	弟	弾
彳	gyō-nin-ben	walk	往	役	彼	待	後
忄(心)	risshin-ben	standing heart	快	性	怖	怪	悔
扌(手)	te-hen	hand	打	投	指	持	拾
方	kata[hō]-hen	direction	旅	族	旋	旗	施
日	hi-hen	day	時	晴	明	暗	昭
木	ki-hen	tree	本	林	村	根	机
氵(水)	sanzui	water	池	活	海	泳	決

火(灬)	hi-hen	fire	灯	炊	炉	畑	焼
牛(牛)	ushi-hen	cow	物	牧	特	牲	牝
犭(犬)	kemono-hen	animal	犯	狂	狩	独	狭
王(玉)	ō-hen (tama-hen)	king (jewel)	理	珍	現	球	望
目	me-hen	eye	眼	眠	眺	睦	瞬
矢	ya-hen	arrow	知	短	矧	矩	矯
石	ishi-hen	stone	研	砂	破	確	硬
礻(示)	shimesu-hen	god	社	神	礼	祈	福
禾	nogi-hen	rice plant	和	利	秋	私	科
米	kome-hen	rice	粒	粋	粗	料	粉
糸	ito-hen	thread	絵	組	細	紙	結
月(肉)	tsuki-hen (niku-zuki)	moon (flesh)	朝	期	勝	服	肝
舟	fune-hen	ship	船	舶	航	般	艇
礻(衣)	koromo-hen	clothing	初	被	裕	補	裸
言	gon-ben	to speak	話	計	記	語	訪

貝	kai-hen	shell	則	販	財	貯	貼
車	kuruma-hen	vehicle	軽	転	輪	輸	軒
金	kane-hen	gold (metal)	針	銀	鉄	鉱	鋭
阝(阜)	kozato-hen	cliff	防	限	降	陽	階
馬	uma-hen	horse	駆	駐	駅	騒	駄
耳	mimi-hen	ear	取	恥	職	聖	聡

▣ Tsukuri (–zukuri): Right-side radical

刀(刂)	katana (rittō)	sword	刈	刊	別	列	判
力	chikara	muscle power	助	加	動	勉	勅
卩	fushi-zukuri	kneeling down	印	危	卵	却	即
彡	san-zukuri	hair of a writing brush; hair style	形	彩	彫	彰	影
攵	boku-nyo	to beat with a club	攻	改	放	教	政
斤	ono-zukuri	ax	斥	新	斬	断	斧
欠	akubi	opened mouth	欧	欣	欲	欺	歌

殳	rumata	weapon	殴	段	殺	殿	穀
阝(邑)	ōzato	walled town	部	都	邦	邪	郊
隹	furutori	bird	集	雇	雄	雅	雑
頁	ōgai	head	頭	頂	順	題	顔

Kammuri: Radical on the top

亠	nabe-buta	pot-lid	交	京	夜	亡	六
冖	wa-kammuri	house (derived from u-kammuri)	写	冗	軍	冠	冥
宀	u-kammuri	house	字	安	客	官	実
癶	hatsu-gashira	to walk slowly and carefully	発	登	癸		
穴	ana-kammuri	hole	空	究	窓	窒	突
竹	take-kammuri	bamboo	答	等	笛	箱	筆
罒(网)	ami-gashira	fowling net	罪	署	置	罰	罷
耂(老)	oi-kammuri	old people	老	孝	考	者	耄
艹	kusa-kammuri	grass	花	芸	苦	若	草

雨	ame-kammuri	rain	雲	雪	電	雷	需

Ashi: Radical at bottom

儿	nin-nyo	people	元	先	兄	充	児
心(忄)	kokoro	heart	思	悪	息	忘	怒
灬(火)	rekka	flame	点	然	無	熱	烈
皿	sara	dish	盆	益	盛	盗	盤
貝	ko-gai	small shell	責	質	貴	貸	買
里	sato	village	野	黒	墨	黙	重

Kamae (-gamae): Fence

冂	dō-gamae	round	円	同	内	再	周
匚	hako-gamae	to settle a matter; to divide	区	医	巨	匹	匠
囗	kuni-gamae	country	国	困	固	団	図
戈	hoko-gamae	halberd	成	我	戒	戦	戯

行	gyō-gamae	to go	術	街	衝	衛	衡
門	mon-gamae	gate	問	聞	開	閉	閣

Tare (–dare): Top and left side

厂	gan-dare	rock of a cliff	反	原	圧	灰	厚
尸	shikabane	roof	局	屋	尽	尼	尾
广	ma-dare	house	広	庫	店	庭	度
疒	yamai-dare	to be sick in bed	病	痛	疲	疫	疾

Nyo [Nyu]: Radical at left and bottom

廴	en-nyo	to walk slowly	廷	建	延	廻	廼
走	sō-nyo	to run	起	超	越	趣	赴
辶	shin-nyo	to advance	近	道	週	進	運

Date: Name: **Exercise Sheet**

● Copy these pages to use as exercise sheets.

Exercise Sheet   Date: Name:

Date: Name: **Exercise Sheet**

Exercise Sheet   Date: Name: